"Then **Junior**
Said to **Jeff...**

The Best NASCAR
Stories Ever Told

David Poole,

Jim McLaurin,

and Tom Gillispie

TRIUMPH
B O O K S

For Leonard Poole, for whom hard work was the story of his life.

—David Poole

For my wife, Inez. Anything short of another War and Peace *fails to do her justice, but for now this'll have to do.*

—Jim McLaurin

For my wife, Holly, who has believed in me all along, and for the late David Poole, who is still with us through this book.

—Tom Gillispie

Library of Congress Cataloging-in-Publication Data

Poole, David, 1959–2009.
  "then Junior said to Jeff" : the best NASCAR stories ever told / David Poole, Jim McLaurin, and Tom Gillispie.
    p. cm.
  ISBN 978-1-60078-767-6
  1. Stock car racing—United States—Anecdotes. 2. NASCAR (Association)—Anecdotes. I. McLaurin, James, 1946– II. Gillispie, Tom. III. Title.
  GV1029.9.S74P65 2012
  796.72092—dc23
  [B]
                                    2012015461

This book is available in quantity at special discounts for your group or organization. For further information, contact:

Triumph Books LLC
814 North Franklin Street
Chicago, Illinois 60610
(312) 337-0747
www.triumphbooks.com

Printed in U.S.A.
ISBN: 978-1-60078-767-6
Design by Patricia Frey
Photos courtesy of AP Images

table of
contents

introduction

If you have a copy of the original *"Then Junior Said to Jeff..."*,
you'll notice that I'm not in it. Jim McLaurin and the late David
Poole wrote it in 2006; at that point, I was a year away from
updating *I Remember Dale Earnhardt* into *Angel in Black:
Remembering Dale Earnhardt Sr.*

But things change. David died in 2009, and Jim is no longer
involved with racing. So Jim contacted me, and I took over the
enjoyable task of updating this edition for Triumph Books.

David Poole and I were friendly, and Jimmy Mac—we all
think of him that way—was my best friend in racing. We often
roomed together at races and on the media tour. In fact, we
roomed together in Atlanta in 1993 during the so-called Storm
of the Century, and I recall us locking arms and sliding down
an icy sidewalk to eat lunch. Just as we hit the bottom of the
little hill, someone opened the door to the dining room, and we
skidded right onto the carpet and walked on in. We stayed
over an extra day or two because we couldn't leave snowed-in
Atlanta.

But there are much better stories here. As Poole pointed
out in the original foreword, the best time to talk to a driver
was often during a rain delay at Darlington or elsewhere. And
sometimes you'll catch a driver in his trailer after practice or
qualifying.

H.A. "Humpy" Wheeler, the former president and promoter
at Charlotte Motor Speedway, still gets that far-off look as he
tells one of his dozens (or hundreds?) of stories. Same with

great storytellers like Buddy Baker, the late Benny Parsons, Darrell Waltrip, Junior Johnson, the late Tim Flock, and others. Flock was especially vivid in his anecdotes and descriptions.

So this book is a sampler of stories Jimmy Mac, Poole, and I have heard and collected over the years.

Jim collected most or all of his stories when he was the long-time auto-racing writer for *The State* newspaper in Columbia, South Carolina. David probably got most of his during his 13 years with the *Charlotte Observer* in North Carolina. I got most of mine in the 1990s when I was working for the *Charleston Post & Courier* in the Lowcountry of South Carolina, and a large number of my best anecdotes came from my freelancing days, also in the '90s, for *Winston Cup Scene*.

After each little section, you'll notice initials. Obviously, J.M. is for Jim McLaurin; D.P. is for David Poole; and T.G. is for Tom Gillispie.

The three of us have brushed on some of the more interesting anecdotes—David called them "heroics and hijinks"—from more than 60 years of NASCAR racing.

This is my fourth book project, and I'm proud to be involved with it. As Poole said in the original foreword, enjoy the ride. And watch out for the pranks, pitfalls, and crashes.

—Tom Gillispie
April 2012

chapter 1
In the Beginning...

Bill Rexford, 1950 NASCAR Strictly Stock Champion, in a practice run, 3-29-51

In the sport's earliest days,
"organized racing" was
almost an oxymoron.

School of Hard Knocks

In racing's formative years, some race promoters were notorious for taking off with the gate receipts before the race, leaving the drivers—whether they liked it or not—to race just for fun.

The drivers themselves were an unruly lot, often making up the rules—and the tracks—as they went. Safety equipment, what there was of it, was rudimentary at best, and more often than not, non-existent.

Long-time racing official Ernie Moore once described a race somewhere in southern Georgia in which "one old boy knocked himself . . . about five times." The race was a 15-lap feature run in a recently harvested cornfield. The "track" quickly deteriorated, Moore said, particularly in one corner.

"There was a hole about 5 feet deep," he remembered. "The cars would hit that hole and the driver's head would bang against the roof of the car. They'd hang out of those cars when they hit that hole. That one old boy knocked himself cuckoo about five times, and every time, he'd crash into another car."

That day, Moore said, the fans saved that driver from himself: "Some of the spectators would pour water on him, and he'd take off again. The fifth time he did it, they didn't bother waking him up." —J.M. (Hunter, pp. 16)

Feels Like the First Time

The first race in what is now known as the NASCAR Sprint Cup Series took place on June 19, 1949, on a three-quarter-mile dirt track in Charlotte, North Carolina.

The track is no longer there—now it's just a field between two highways near the city's airport. But on that afternoon, a 150-mile race on a rutted track that took its toll on man and machine gave birth to what is now America's premier motorsports series.

The idea was to have cars come straight to the race track from off the showroom floor. The name of the series outlined the rulebook—it was NASCAR's new "strictly stock" series that had its first official race scheduled for that day.

The drivers were allowed to make only the most minor adjustments—removing wheel covers and adding seat belts, things like that. Many drivers went to military surplus stores and got belts to tie themselves in, while others simply used, well, belts, the ones they used to hold their pants up.

There were 33 cars entered. One was driven by a young man from Denton, North Carolina, named Archie Smith.

"It cost $25 to enter," Smith recalls. "Nobody had that. I was working for 75¢ an hour and my daddy didn't want me to go. But he finally agreed to loan me the money."

Smith had heard about the race in a radio advertisement. Jim Roper, who was from Kansas, had read about it in a comic strip in his local newspaper and made the long drive. That would turn out to be a good decision.

Smith brought his personal car down to Charlotte, taped up the headlights, buckled the doors closed with a leather belt, and strapped himself in with an old horse harness he bought at a hardware store.

But first, he made a little side trip.

"I wanted to be smarter than anybody else," Smith says. "We went to the airport and filled up with airplane gas. They came out and caught us and wanted to know what we were doing. We told them we were buying gas for the race. They were about to make us pump it all out."

But just before the race started, Smith's car would not start. He had a buddy, who was helping him in the pits, paged over the public address system. The friend brought an air tank and he and Smith blew out the gas lines and started the race.

Drivers weren't the only ones who'd heard about the race, of course. A boy living just across the Catawba River in the town of Belmont knew there was a race that day, so he walked from Belmont Abbey College, where his father was the athletics director, down to the intersection of US 74 and hitchhiked his way to the show. The young man, Howard Wheeler, later picked up the same nickname his father had: Humpy.

Archie Smith wasn't the only North Carolina driver to come to the state's largest city to race that day, either. Lee Petty drove down from Level Cross with two carloads of family and friends.

One of the cars was the one Lee raced in the event. During the race, he hooked a tire in one of the ruts the heavy cars had worn into the track's surface and flipped it. Not only did that end Petty's race, it also rendered one of the cars the Petty clan had used to get to Charlotte unworthy of making the trip back home. So after the race, the womenfolk took the working car home. Lee stayed back in Charlotte to get the other car fixed. And his young son, Richard, hitchhiked home.

When the checkered flag flew after 200 laps, Glenn Dunnaway from nearby Gastonia was the winner.

Or was he?

The springs in the 1947 Ford that Dunnaway drove had been altered. And since this was a strictly stock race, that was illegal.

So Roper, the Kansan who'd literally seen it in the funny papers, was declared the winner. —D.P.

Racing Like a Lady

To the everlasting delight of the automobile racing crowd, Louise Smith talked as good a game as she played.

"You had to fight all the time," Smith once said. "I thought men weren't supposed to hit women and women weren't supposed to hit men, but I found out it went both ways. If you won a race, you just about had to fight."

A Greenville, South Carolina, native, Smith was born in 1916 and was one of the true pioneers in racing. She was a racer before there was a NASCAR, winning 38 races in the modified division in the 1940s and '50s.

She managed to catch the eye of a young promoter named Bill France and, when she finished third in her first race at Greenville-Pickens Speedway, she and France figured they had a good thing.

"Coming in third made a lot of them mad," she said. "I think a lot of them are mad at me now. . . . But Bill France and I became good friends, and he let me race. I think I turned out to be a pretty good driver."

Racing was a novelty in itself in the early days, and Smith's presence in a male-dominated sport may have been looked at as a gimmick. But her opponents came to know her as a hard-knocking competitor who gave as good as she took.

"I let them push me around to start with," she said, "but Buddy Shuman...we were in Asheville and all out at a party one night—a big racing shebang with them and their wives—and he came up and told me he wanted to take me out to the speedway the next morning and show me something.

"He took me out to Weaverville Speedway and showed me how to bump them on the back fender and make them flip [spin out]. We practiced that thing all day Saturday, and I got to where I could do it pretty good.

"He got killed that night, but I got to where they called me 'Little Buddy Shuman' after that. I didn't have to hit but two guys who were hitting on me. I cut them a flip, and nobody didn't bother me no more."

In 1999 Smith was voted into the International Motorsports Hall of Fame at Talladega, Alabama. As of 2005, she was still one of only two women (drag racing legend Shirley Muldowney being the other) in the Hall.

She was as tough a competitor as there was in racing's wild and wooly days, gender be damned.

"They were all rough," she said. "I don't know who was the roughest. We were all friends, but once you hit that race track, you ain't got no friends.

"It's every man for hisself. And on my part, it was every woman for hisself." —J.M.

Oops!

Long before Danica Patrick, Lyn St. James, or Janet Guthrie, there was Louise Smith. She was hell on wheels, but she had her share of wrecks.

Her first automobile accident was with her daddy's Model T. The tot took the wheel, couldn't stop the car, and drove it right into the chicken coop.

Then she had her racing wrecks.

Once in Hillsborough, North Carolina, Curtis Turner was teaching her how to slide a car through the turns on a dirt track, then apply the gas as she left the corners. She broke the track record in qualifying, but on her third circuit, the car went airborne and wiped out some small trees. They cut her out of the wreckage with a torch; she needed 48 stitches, and four pins were inserted in her left knee.

Her signature wreck, though, came in 1947. She took Noah's new Ford coupe to Daytona Beach to watch the beach races, but she wanted to race. So she raced the new car and, naturally, wrecked it. She didn't want to tell Noah. She got home, and when he asked about the car, she said it broke down in Augusta, Georgia.

Then he showed her the local newspaper and the front-page photo of his crumpled coupe.

Oops. —T.G.

X Marks the Spot

Francis Eduardo Menendez, better known as Frank Mundy because his buddies in his hometown of Atlanta found that easier to pronounce than the former, made a couple of marks in NASCAR in its formative years.

But he was better known as a stunt car driver. Mundy spent seven years with Lucky Teter's Hell Drivers and became an expert at somersaulting a car, jumping it 120', and crashing it head-on. Especially crashing it head-on.

"I volunteered for the head-on crash because it paid $10 more a week," Mundy said. "The secret to a perfect head-on was to be able to drive the car from the back seat. You ducked behind a mattress just before impact."

Mundy won three races on NASCAR's Grand National circuit, and he even won the pole for the second Southern 500 at Darlington—in a Studebaker—in 1951.

But he cut his racing teeth at the old Lakewood Speedway in Atlanta in the pre–World War II era. "I was knocked cold only once on a track, and it came in those early days at Lakewood," he said.

Lakewood was a dirt oval with a lake in the infield, and one of the dustier tracks around.

"The stockers kicked up so much dust you couldn't see the other cars," Mundy said. "Anytime you drive blind, you drive scared. I was judging the turns on the backstretch by a bunch of trees. When I saw them, I'd count to five or six and then straighten the car. I was busy counting when I plowed into six other cars who must have been counting, too.

"I woke up in the ambulance. After they found no broken bones, I raced back, borrowed a car, and finished second in the feature." .

Mundy was one of the few drivers of that era who flew to races and let whoever he was driving for haul the car to the track. That semi-backfired on him in 1956, when he arrived at a track near Los Angeles to find his car hadn't made it.

He rented a car, painted an X on the door, and finished eighth in the race without a pit crew, extra tires, or gas. He won $100, and the car rental only came to $37, so Mundy still came out ahead. —J.M. (Cutter, pp. 432–33)

Long Time Running

Dick Rathmann's win in a 250-lap race at California's Oakland Speedway in 1954 was the first last-place-to-first-place victory in NASCAR history, but that's not the half of it.

Rathmann's journey to the checkered flag was more like a marathon than a 125-mile sprint.

Rathmann, a Californian who had come east to race stock cars, and his mechanic Jim Ellis picked up a brand new Hudson Hornet race car in Atlanta, Georgia, four days before the race to haul it out to California. The pair took turns sleeping while the other one drove, at one point motoring through a snowstorm, until they were about 100 miles from Oakland.

Then the car they were using to tow the race car broke down. Rathmann decided to use the race car to tow the other car to the track, and he and Ellis arrived at 1:00 AM on the day of the race. They spent the morning getting the race car in shape for qualifying and then, during his qualifying lap, the gas tank fell off, evidently having been weakened by towing the tow car, and it was unlikely that they would find a replacement.

However, another Hudson just like Rathmann's crashed during qualifying and destroyed everything on the car *but* the gas tank. Rathmann borrowed the tank and made it into the field, taking the 26th (and last) qualifying spot.

By then, the crowd had gotten wind of his extraordinary efforts in just getting to the race, and they cheered wildly as he took the lead on lap 143 and led the rest of the way.

After the race, someone pointed out to Rathmann that it had taken him less than 2½ hours (2 hours, 27 minutes, and 57 seconds) to finish the race.

A weary Rathmann smiled and said it felt more like a week.
—J.M. (Engel, pp. 106)

chapter 2
Curtis and Smokey and Harry and 'Em

Curtis Turner in 1966 Chevy (13) runs off track at Daytona on 2-26-67

NASCAR history is replete with colorful characters, men who've made their mark on the sport in many ways.

Well Suited to the Task

Curtis Turner made and lost several fortunes in the timber business, and no doubt could have won more NASCAR races if he'd approached racing differently. But it was said that if Turner did lose a race, he never lost a party.

Turner's parties were legendary affairs that sometimes lasted for days, and when one was over, his favorite phrase was, "There's another party startin' in 15 minutes."

On the race track, Turner's philosophy was that if it took beating and banging to get to the front—indeed, he once won a race in Asheville, North Carolina, when his was the only car left running at the end—then all the better.

The venue changes occasionally, as does the color of the suit, but Turner once drove a race in a three-piece business suit—the result of having shown up late for a race with a crushing hangover.

Or, depending on who was telling the story, about half-smashed.

"I was about half-tuned when I got to the race and didn't even have time to change my clothes," Turner himself said. "So I just got in the car with my suit and tie on and took off runnin'. Blew a tire and finished fourth.

"I told my sponsors they ought to want their drivers to dress like gentlemen." —J.M. (Chapin, pp. 41)

The Honor System?

Country and western star Marty Robbins loved racing as much as he did singing, often leaving the Grand Ole Opry show as soon as his number was over to go out to the speedway in Nashville to beat and bang with the locals.

If he didn't have an engagement, he sometimes followed the show on the road.

Racing was his hobby. And while he didn't have the money it took to run up front, he enjoyed racing back in the pack with the rest of the "independents."

Well, except maybe once.

In 1972 at Talladega Superspeedway, Robbins surprised even himself by going a lot faster than he'd ever gone, certainly faster than NASCAR had expected him to. Late in the race, he was clocked at 188 mph, when he had only qualified at 177. He finished 18th in the race.

Even he suspected something fishy, so he asked NASCAR technical inspector Bill Gazaway to have a look at his carburetor. Someone had given him one that was a trifle larger than it should have been.

Robbins refused the $250 bonus for being the highest-finishing rookie in the race, and NASCAR disqualified him for the illegal carburetor. The incident cost him more than $1,000.

Robbins didn't care, saying that it was worth it just to see the look on Joe Frasson's face when he blew by. —J.M.

No Taxi Driver

Benny Parsons was known as the racing cab driver, but it's not really true.

Here's how it came about: Benny's parents, Harold and Hazel, took Benny's younger brother, Phil, and moved to Detroit to make a living. Benny stayed behind to live with Julia Parsons, the young Benny's beloved great-grandmother. Eventually, he joined the family in Detroit, where they had a gas station and a cabstand, and he mostly worked on cabs but occasionally drove one if needed.

When Benny filled out an application for a NASCAR license, he wrote "taxicab business" where it said "occupation." From then on, he was stuck with being called "the racing cab driver." —T.G.

Just a Guy Doing His Job

Sam McQuagg, who raced on NASCAR's Grand National circuit in the 1960s, might be best remembered as the other guy in the photo when Cale Yarborough jumped the fence at Darlington in 1965.

But McQuagg did have his one day in the sun.

McQuagg, in fact, was more remarkable by the fact that there was little remarkable about him in an era when bigger-than-life heroes such as Yarborough, David Pearson, and Richard Petty ruled racing.

McQuagg was the son of a carpenter from Columbus, Georgia, and was a man of simple pleasures. Devoted to his wife, McQuagg did not race on Friday nights because that's when he took her out to dinner. Once, when asked why he would not attend a racing dinner on Sunday evening, he said, "My favorite TV program, *Bonanza*, is on, and I wouldn't miss it for the world."

In 1965 McQuagg won rookie of the year honors for five top-10 finishes in 15 races, and the Chrysler camp steered him into a highly regarded Ray Nichels Dodge for the next season. When the circuit got to Daytona, Florida, in July for the Firecracker 400, he put it all together.

He charged into the lead for the first nine laps, then settled in until it was time to race. He battled Jim Paschal, Buddy Baker, and even the legendary Curtis Turner until taking the lead for good for the final 30 laps.

It turned out to be the only major-league win of his career, but he celebrated in typical McQuagg fashion: he took his wife out to a nice steak house in Daytona, then drove all the way back to Columbus.

The next morning he was out at dawn, delivering papers for a neighborhood boy who was sick. Maybe in part because the banner headline in his hometown paper read: McQuagg Wins at Daytona.

"It was great for my garage business," he said. —J.M.

Jocko and Flock

Tim Flock was pretty calm when he told me the story of Jocko Flocko, a Rhesus monkey that was Tim's co-pilot for eight races in 1953. Still, Flock had a gleam in his eye as he talked.

On May 16, 1953, Jocko rode with Flock as the future Hall of Famer won the Grand National race at Hickory Motor Speedway in North Carolina.

It started out as a publicity stunt, and Flock gave Jocko his own driving suit and a special seat. The stunt ended two weeks later with the Raleigh 300 in Raleigh, North Carolina.

The cars in those days had trap doors so that the driver could pull a chain and check for tire wear. During the Raleigh

300, Jocko squirmed out of his seat and stuck his head through the trap door.

Naturally, Jocko went ape.

"It was hard enough to drive those heavy old cars back then under normal circumstances," Flock said, "but with a crazed monkey clawing you at the same time, it becomes nearly impossible!"

Flock raced into the pits, put Jocko out, went back, and finished third.

"The pit stop cost me second place and a $600 difference in my paycheck. Jocko was retired immediately," Flock said. "I had to get that monkey off my back!"

Flock had a good season in '53, with one win and 18 top-10s, but in 1955 he had NASCAR's first really big season, winning 18 of 39 races.

Postscript: In the late 1990s, I came across a short-track driver in South Carolina who carried toy monkeys in the back window of his Late Model car. Naturally, I thought of Jocko, and I believe that man won the track championship that year. —T.G. (TimFlock.com)

"Hey, Look Where You're Walking"

Cale Yarborough was still a kid the first time he raced at Daytona, in a modified race, but he found out that he had arrived. Not because he'd led the race, but because he was invited to Robinson's, a bar on South Atlantic Avenue where all the hotshot racers hung out.

Curtis Turner and Joe Weatherly, two of the wildest party men in racing, frequented the place because their "party pad" was right across the street.

About midway through his first evening at Robinson's, Yarborough said he was approached by a well-tuned Turner, who invited him to stop by anytime. Yarborough was impressed, but he didn't know quite what to make of the invitation. He noted that the "pad" was more than a little rundown and wondered aloud why two such big-time drivers as Turner and Weatherly would stay in such a shabby hostelry when they could have afforded any place on the beach.

"Well, kid," Turner told him, "when I get ready to go home at night, I figure the worst thing that can happen to me is someone might step on my fingers." —J.M. (Yarborough, Neely, pp. 139)

The Best Damn Storyteller in Town

Henry "Smokey" Yunick was the most innovative auto mechanic racing has ever seen, and maybe the best storyteller of them all.

In the latter years of his life (he succumbed to cancer in 2001), Yunick could be seen occasionally around media centers at race tracks, scribbling on legal-length pads.

What many did not know at the time was that he was writing his life history. And what tales he told. When he was finished, the result was a three-volume set of largely unedited (at his behest) copy that told it like it was, at least in his eyes.

The difference between yesterday's and today's race car drivers?

"Yesterday's driver was a social disaster," said Yunick, whose legendary Daytona Beach garage was known as "The Best Damn Garage in Town."

"He drank too much and much of his time was consumed in personal problems, usually female-oriented…. Hell, if you went to a hotel for a room and filled in the 'occupation' blank with, 'racer,' suddenly the hotel was out of rooms…. Today's racer is a whole new ball game. Probably has the highest social rating going in all of the entertainment venues….

"Hell, a 'Winston Cupper' without a jet is hurting, the driver with a turbo-prop is looked down on. I can remember when the sign of success was when the car company of the make you race loaned you a new car to drive."

Women drivers?

"I know this is gonna piss a lot of people off, but I've never seen a good 'big time circle racing female.' I've seen females with super skill, but I never saw one that could race. No big deal as I see it; I never saw a male have a baby."

Don't even ask about Bill France Jr., who rated marginally lower than Bill Sr. in Yunick's estimation.

"When Billy came back from the Army, he did something that ticked me off. I was complaining about it to his dad. I said, 'It will take him five years in the fifth grade to get an idiot's license.'

"Big Bill said, 'I think he can do it in four.'" —J.M.

A Two-Sided Bud Car

In 1984 or so, car owner Junior Johnson got the bright idea of putting the same sponsor on two cars, something that wasn't so common at the time. He already had No. 11 cars for Darrell Waltrip, and he wanted to add a No. 12 team for Neil Bonnett.

The problem was that Junior's team didn't have any No. 12 cars, so they had to start building.

Their biggest problem probably came when they had to do preseason publicity photos. With no 12 car handy, Junior got creative. He had his folks paint up one Budweiser car for both teams, with No. 11 on one door and No. 12 on the other. DW's team posed for photos with one door, and then Bonnett's crew posed with the other.

Someone should have covered up the number on the top of the car when they were shooting from the wrong side, but apparently they didn't think of that.

"If you look at the roof of the car in those pictures, it's pretty obvious what we were up to," Johnson said. "Luckily, not a lot people noticed. Everything looked normal in the pictures, but it was pretty crazy."

And crazy fit Johnson's two teams perfectly.

"Looking back, you might say that was kind of fitting," said Jeff Hammond, then Waltrip's crew chief. "Because from the outside, everything might have looked normal about that two-car team. But the reality was it was pretty crazy, too."

The highlight for the two-car team probably came in 1984 during the Cup race at the .596-mile oval at the Tennessee State Fairgrounds in Nashville. Waltrip won the pole and led the first 43 laps. Bonnett started 15th and was leading by lap 87. In the final 200 laps, Bonnett led all but 13 laps and was ahead with 10 laps to go. Geoff Bodine took the lead for three laps. Then with seven laps left, Waltrip took the lead for the fourth time, but Bonnett was on his tailpipe.

A yellow flag flew on lap 418, bringing out a well-timed caution.

On the final lap, Bonnett passed Waltrip and took the checkered flag first. The late Dick Beaty, then the series director, declared Bonnett the winner, but Waltrip quickly disagreed with the ruling and argued that the rulebook agreed with him.

"The caution flag was out when we got to the finish line on the next-to-last lap," an incensed DW said. "I had beaten Neil back to the line. I won the race at that point. He can't pass me when the yellow flag is out."

The rulebook said that "when the yellow flag is displayed during the white-flag lap, all cars will be scored on the basis of the position in which the cars cross the start-finish line after receiving the checkered flag."

After two days of review, NASCAR finally agreed that the caution flag had waved before Waltrip took the white flag and before Bonnett made his last-lap pass. Therefore, Bonnett's pass was not legal. Waltrip got the win, and Bonnett was shifted back to second.

The bottom line: if Bonnett had gotten the win, Waltrip would have been tied with Cale Yarborough with 83 victories rather than being tied with Bobby Allison with 84, fourth on the all-time win list. —T.G. (ESPN.com and Motor Racing Network)

"Just Sign on the Dotted Line, Billy..."

When Curtis Turner and fellow entrepreneur Bruton Smith attempted to build Charlotte Motor Speedway, both got in a little deeper than they'd hoped.

In the early 1960s the two men, neither of whom really trusted the other, entered into a shaky agreement to build a

$2 million track in Concord, North Carolina. Underfinanced from the outset, the venture was in deep trouble when Turner went to the Teamsters Union to ask for an $850,000 loan to complete the work. In return, Turner would attempt to organize the drivers into a union.

NASCAR president Bill France Sr. hated unions and saw them as a threat to his stranglehold on racing. He banned Turner and Tim Flock, who also was working to organize the drivers, for life.

France eventually reinstated both drivers, and Smith left racing for a few years to make a fortune in the automobile dealership business before he returned to buy out the other shareholders of Charlotte Motor Speedway. It became the foundation for his racing empire.

But when their fate hung in the balance, France called a meeting of the drivers and mechanics—everybody except Turner and Flock—in August 1961 before a race at Winston-Salem, North Carolina.

Turner was standing outside the building where the meeting was going on, and he overheard Big Bill say that if the unions were all they were cracked up to be, he'd join himself.

"I was outside the window," Turner said later, "and I raised it up and handed him a card through the window and said, 'Here's your application.' They closed the window on me. From then on, it was just lawyers and lawsuits." —J.M. (Chapin, pp. 94)

Things Change

The year was 1989, and Richard Petty was the King in name only.

Petty's record streak of 513 straight starts had ended the previous week at Richmond, and Richard had just qualified a distant 38th at Rockingham (he'd finish 16th on Sunday). A young sportswriter stopped him for a couple of questions, and the King of NASCAR glared down at his tormentor.

Petty, whose 200th (and last) victory had come nearly five years before this, must have realized his run was about to end.

He'd race three more seasons, of course, but he wasn't a royal driver anymore. In fact, NASCAR would adopt a special former champion's provisional spot just so Petty could make race fields. Ironically, it was the 43rd spot in the field, matching the King's famous car number.

But that was in the future. The writer wanted to know why Petty was struggling. After some self-analysis and a little bluster, Petty admitted that things change. People change. Drivers change. You're not as reckless in your forties and fifties as you are in your twenties and thirties. Fame seems less important; life becomes more precious.

He said he had to worry more about his family than qualifying.

When he was asked what he meant, he asked the writer if he was married. "No, I'm not," the writer said. Petty, now his normal self, smiled sadly, and patted the man on the shoulder.

"You'll learn," he said. "You'll learn."

The next year, he talked more about a driver changing. He said that his biggest problem was too much information. He said a young driver would see a wreck, pick a hole, and dive through it (or plow into someone else). Petty said that, then in his fifties, he'd immediately use his vast knowledge and try to decide where to go. Before he'd pick a hole, he'd often just pile into somebody. —T.G.

First in Wrecks

Richard Petty is the King of NASCAR, and he leads in so many categories.

But Lee Petty has two things over his son, one positive, one negative.

While Richard won a record seven Daytona 500s, Lee won the first Daytona 500, beating Johnny Beauchamp in a photo finish that took two or three days to determine.

He's also credited with being the first driver to crash in a NASCAR race. He wrecked his family Buick on lap 107 in the first NASCAR race, held in Charlotte, North Carolina, on June 19, 1949.

He started ninth and was credited with a 17th-place finish among 33 cars. He won $25.

His season—six starts in eight NASCAR Strictly Stock starts—ended better. He finished second at Martinsville, first at Pittsburgh, and second at North Wilkesboro. —T.G.

Langley Shows the Legends How

When Ralph Seagraves, the R.J. Reynolds Tobacco salesman who was largely responsible for putting the "Winston" in NASCAR's Winston Cup, was given the honor to say

"Gentlemen, start your engines!" before the first (and as it turned out, last) Winston Legends race at Lowe's Motor Speedway, the fans should have known they were in for a treat.

Instead of the traditional command, Seagraves said, "I've raced with these guys for 30 years, and there ain't a gentleman among 'em. Fire 'em up!"

What followed on the specially built half-mile track on the track's front straightaway was 30 laps of racing the way it used to be. Only 11 of the 22 heroes from NASCAR's past who started the race finished it, and even those cars were only recognizable by the paint schemes.

The drivers competed in modern-day race cars, but with the numbers and colors they had made famous in NASCAR's early days. When they were finished, the numbers and paint schemes were about the only thing that distinguished them from fodder for the junkyard.

With guys like Buck Baker, Junior Johnson, and Cale Yarborough in the field, who would have expected less?

Johnson, the one-time bootleg runner who was known as one of the hardest-driving competitors in racing history, was involved in several skirmishes—one of which was with the pace car, which was driven by former NASCAR president Bill France Jr.

Elmo Langley raced his entire career as a field-filler, always in under-funded equipment and with only two victories in what became NASCAR's Winston Cup Series. Until 1991, that is.

Relegated to driving NASCAR's pace car in his post-retirement years, Langley had the honor of facing the best of the best one last time, and he showed them how it was done.

Langley nudged three-time champion Yarborough out of the way on the final lap to take the checkered flag.

"I got Cale on the last lap, and I didn't have any reason to back off," he said.

Yarborough took the loss with more good grace than usual, saying, "He caught me napping. I didn't even see him until he passed me." —J.M.

The Wreck on the Road Course

I've collected a lot of stories over the years, and a few of them came from T. Wayne Robertson, who died in a boating accident in 1998, and Neil Bonnett, who died during practice at Daytona in 1994.

Wayne started out driving show cars for R.J. Reynolds and Winston.

Wayne was a wonderful conversationalist, and he knew everyone in racing. He liked to tell stories of being the Winston Cup pace car driver, including one where David Pearson pushed the pace car from behind and got Wayne up to 130 mph entering the turn.

His eyes twinkled and bulged out at the same time as he told it.

In another, there was a famous incident where Bobby Allison was leading at Nashville under caution, and Bobby thought he was a lap ahead of the field. So he tried to pass the pace car under caution! Bobby would try to get around Wayne, who would put on the block. Allison almost pushed Wayne—and the pace car—off the track.

Bobby, who has had memory problems stemming from a 1988 wreck at Pocono, told me that he didn't remember the pace car battle, but Wayne sure did.

Oddly, Neil and Wayne told me the same story from two different perspectives. They were at the road course in Riverside, California, and Neil said he always had trouble in a certain turn; I remember it as Turn 7, but it could have been anywhere.

The way Neil told it—it was close to Wayne's version— Wayne and a friend of his were going to wait in this turn, and Neil told Wayne to watch out, that he was going to wreck in that turn.

"I was bustin' ass through there, making good time," Bonnett said, "and I got to that turn, and I saw Wayne and his friend. I lost my concentration and slid off the track. As I was re-firing the engine, I could see Wayne and his friend with their jaws dropping a foot.

"It was almost worth it to wreck!"—T.G.

"Pops, Are We Flying Yet?"

In addition to being a daring driver, Curtis Turner's exploits in the cockpit of an airplane are equally as legendary.

One story involved his running mate "Little" Joe Weatherly, and demonstrated Turner's utter lack of fear—and maybe common sense—in the left-hand seat of anything.

It seems that once he was running late for a race at Darlington, so instead of flying his private plane into the local airport, he attempted to land it on the track's backstretch.

That was not so much a problem. Getting out was another story.

Since the backstretch of the old track was only some 1,300' long—with two-story banking in Turn 3 to clear—taking off would have been a hair-raising task even for an astronaut.

The way Weatherly remembered the story, when Turner got ready to leave, he asked "Little" Joe if he wanted to fly with him. Perhaps the only man in Christendom as crazy as Turner, Weatherly said he'd do it.

Since it would take all of Turner's concentration to get the plane off the ground in such a short space, he asked his pal if he'd take care of raising the landing gear.

Turner built up a little speed through the first and second turns, then when he hit the backstretch, he gunned it. As the plane roared down the back straightaway headed for the mountainous turn, Turner looked over at his co-pilot and asked, "Pops, are we flyin' yet?"

Weatherly looked over at the commander and replied, "I hope so. I lifted the landing gear a long time ago." —J.M. (McLaurin, pp. 117–18)

Cale and No. 200

Cale Yarborough had a chance to really screw up Richard Petty's NASCAR legend in the 1984 Pepsi 400 at Daytona. President Reagan was in attendance, and Petty, in a three-year skid, was going for victory No. 200. Yarborough had won his fourth Daytona 500 that year from the pole and was seeking a season sweep at the track, and he was on the pole for the Daytona summer race.

They were racing to the caution flag; whoever got there first would win under caution.

"I had Richard set up for a slingshot move," Yarborough once told me, "but the caution came out with two laps to go. I wasn't in the right position to make it work completely, but I had to make a run because I knew the race would be over when we got around to the flag. I had him beat in (Turns) 3 and 4, but I didn't have enough momentum. He beat me by a foot."

Most people don't realize that Cale didn't finish second. Harry Gant inherited second after Yarborough went down pit road, mistakenly thinking the race was over at lap 158. Cale got third that day.

But all turned out well. Petty's 200 victories sound a lot better than 199. —T.G.

Gant Outruns Everything but the Fish

"Handsome" Harry Gant was one of the best race car drivers to ever grab a steering wheel but, as it turns out, he was not a half-bad fisherman, either. In a story passed along to veteran racing writer Tom Higgins by 1973 NASCAR Winston Cup champion Benny Parsons, Gant proved he was as handy with a rod and reel as he was with a race car.

After Parsons won the 1984 Coca-Cola 500 in Atlanta, Lou Bantle, the president of U.S. Tobacco Co. (which sponsored Parsons' Leo Jackson–owned car) wanted to reward all his drivers, which included Gant and Parsons' brother Phil, with something special. He arranged a fishing trip to a nice fishing lodge near Willingham, Alaska. What Bantle didn't know was that none of his guests were fishermen, but they were too polite to mention the fact.

On about the third day of the trip, according to Parsons, the entire party was fishing a shallow, wide part of the Wood River, and Gant waded out to about the middle of the run.

"He immediately begins catching rainbow trout after rainbow trout that look about as long as your arm," Parsons said. "He's releasing the fish after netting them.

"It gets so ridiculous that Harry starts counting, rubbing it in on the rest of us, who aren't having anywhere near that kind of luck. 'Twelve trout in 12 casts! Thirteen trout in 13 casts!' and right on. He gets up to eighteen and suddenly quits fishing."

"Harry then heads toward the bank, explaining that 'There ain't nothing to this.' Harry grinned and said, 'I'm gonna take me a nap.'"

As Gant waded to the shore with his rod over his shoulder, somehow or other he accidentally pushed the button on his reel and his lure dropped into the water.

"So help me, another trout grabs that spinner and the rod tip starts jerking down over Harry's shoulder. He spins around, sets the hook, and starts yelling, 'Nineteen in a row! Nineteen in a row!'

"As Harry comes by me he winks and says, 'I've got to get out of this river. They're chasing me!'" —J.M.

NASCAR's Historian

I met Robert Graham "Bob" Latford in 1990. I had just become the auto-racing writer for what is now the *Charleston*

(South Carolina) Post and Courier, and my predecessor
suggested I look up Bob Latford, the resident racing historian. I
found the tall, older man with a handlebar mustache, a big
smile, and a pack of cigarettes in the sleeve of his short-
sleeved shirt. I'd also found a friend.

Latford got into racing in the late 1940s, when he sold
programs on the beach-road course at Daytona. Later, he
became the public relations director for a couple of racetracks.
When we met, he was doing PR for Junior Johnson. Later, he
did a newsletter that was called *The Inside Line*. It was a good
play on words, and, although it was written in an archaic style,
it was big on facts.

Sometimes, he'd run the media center or press box for a
racetrack, and you'd see him moderating press conferences.
He was always quick to say that someone missed making the
race by $26/1,000^{th}$ of a second or say that the field qualified
less than a half-second from first to last. And we'd dutifully
write it down.

His claim to fame, I guess, was the fact that he helped
design the NASCAR points system at an eating/drinking
establishment in Daytona Beach. Legend has it that the system
was written on a napkin.

When he died on July 23, 2003, Bob got the final ticks of
his 15 minutes of fame. NASCAR's point system was coming
under fire for the umpteenth time, and people were writing
about it. Many said Latford invented the system.

When we first talked about it in the early '90s, Bob said
he was one of four or five in attendance. Bill Gazaway, then
the Winston Cup director, was there. Bill France Sr. was
there, too. In the last few years, Bob began to say, "When I

developed the point system…," and I didn't contradict him. Bob had a way of changing his stories, and I guess this was one of them.

He *was* a changeable sort. One time, he'd say they ought to give five extra points for a win and five points for a pole. Next time, he'd say five more for the win and none for a pole. The third time, he'd say they ought to keep it the way it is.

The fact that Latford didn't create the point system is irrelevant. He *did* help create it. Many people give him credit for the system that's been used for years to get information to the media. He was a gold mine of stories and information and opinions.

And he had a big smile amidst a swirl of cranky reporters, racing noise, and cigarette smoke. Of course, Bob often was the source of the smoke. —T.G.

chapter 3
The Lady in Black

Southern 500 at Darlington Raceway, 8-31-03

Darlington Raceway is NASCAR's version of Fenway Park or Wrigley Field, a place where the history comes at you like waves crashing on the beach.

Sleep Tight and Don't Let the Bed Bugs Bite

The first Southern 500 at the track in South Carolina came on Labor Day of 1950, and seen through the light of over a half a century of NASCAR racing, it was perhaps the most pivotal stock car race in history.

In the first place, no one knew if cars right off the showroom floor would last 500 miles racing under the harsh conditions of a Sandlapper summer.

None of the drivers had ever seen a track like the 1¼-mile monster that local entrepreneur Harold Brasington had carved out of a peanut patch, much less raced on one.

But if the race had a jolting effect on racing, imagine what it meant to the townspeople who had never seen such a crowd of people. Darlington, South Carolina, was a quiet little hamlet of a few thousand souls when some 25,000 race fans poured in. The town, which boasted only one motel, was, to put it mildly, swamped.

Some of the reporters who came in to cover the race were lucky enough to find dorm rooms available at Coker College in nearby Hartsville, and there were a few motels in Florence, 10 miles away. But most people stayed wherever they found a spot to lay their heads. Hundreds slept under the stars on the town square.

Bud Moore, who owned two cars that were entered in the race—Joe Eubanks in a Mercury and Harold Kite in a Lincoln— found out soon enough that his lofty status was no guarantee of a room.

"We slept in the cars at the race track," Moore said. "We didn't have hotels and didn't have the money to pay for a hotel, anyway.

"I remember going to the hotel downtown. We went upstairs and went in the room. I turned the covers back and saw the biggest black bug you've ever seen. I told Joe Eubanks, 'Dogged if I can sleep in this bed with all these bugs.'

"We went downstairs and I told the guy behind the counter that I couldn't sleep in there with all those bugs. He said, 'Them bugs won't bite. They'll go to sleep, too.'

"We slept in the car that night." —J.M.

Joltin' Joe has Left and Gone Away...

If life was exciting for the adults in Darlington in the days leading up to that first Southern 500, imagine what it must have been like to be a kid. Especially if your dad was the man responsible for putting Darlington on the map.

Harold Brasington Jr. was nine years old when William H. G. "Big Bill" France rolled into town that summer and, being closer to the action than most, he reveled in the reflected glory.

France was a tall, garrulous man of the sort Harold Jr. had never seen. Since there were no motel rooms available anywhere near Darlington, France bunked in with the Brasingtons, and young Harold must have thought he was in heaven.

For some reason, the younger Brasington said many years later, France wanted to talk to New York Yankees great Joe DiMaggio. It fell to the young boy to get him on the phone—

this was in the pre-dial days, and to place a long distance call, you had to talk to the local operator.

"You can imagine how excited a nine-year-old kid was when he told me that," Brasington said. "I pick up the phone. The operator says, 'Can I help you?' I said, 'I'd like to speak to Joe DiMaggio.'

"She said, 'Honey, so would I,' and hung up."

But young Brasington was as tenacious as his dad, and he kept after the operator until she actually got the baseball legend on the phone.

"Then," he said, "I took my friends to my house and said, 'Joe DiMaggio talked on this telephone.'" —J.M.

Too Bad for Buck

Buck Baker was a city bus driver in Charlotte, North Carolina, but he also was a great race car driver. He won two NASCAR championships, in 1956 and 1957, and won the Southern 500 at Darlington three times in his career.

In the first Southern 500, however, Baker crashed his car badly in a big wreck and, for at least a few minutes, people thought he'd been badly hurt or killed.

That race was the first 500-mile race—anywhere—for stock cars. It was Labor Day weekend in the Pee Dee of South Carolina, where heat and humidity have a summer home. Some people thought cars couldn't last for 500 miles that day, and even more thought the drivers might not be able to withstand the heat for that duration.

The drivers, being a hardy lot, were determined to prove them wrong.

Most took something cold to drink with them in their cars to help them go the distance, and Baker's choice was a gallon jug of cold tomato juice.

When his car got wrecked, the first person who came to check on Baker looked inside and recoiled in horror. "No need to bother with Baker," he said. "The poor guy has had his head cut off."

Actually, Baker wasn't hurt at all. It wasn't his blood all over the place inside the car.

It was tomato juice. —D.P.

The Wet Spot

Take my word for it: David Pearson was (and probably still is) a prankster. I once was walking by when Pearson, then retired, snuck into the Wood Brothers' garage area at Rockingham, threw a hose in there, and yelled, "Snake!" You could hear crewmen bumping around, apparently trying to get away, with a gleeful David skulking out the way he came.

He pulled another prank in 2008 when Darlington Raceway held the Darlington Historic Racing Festival and brought in big names like Pearson, Junior Johnson, Darrell Waltrip, Marvin Panch, Ray Fox, and more.

He was giving track rides, and he wanted to make it look like people had peed themselves from all the speed. Relax, David's a professional; he surely had done this before.

"At one point when the track was cold, David Pearson wanted to give track rides around the track. They had a replica 21 Wood Brothers Purolator car," said Chris Browning, the president of Darlington Raceway. "We said, 'Yeah, sure. We're pretty much done for the day. We'll let everybody know. Go on and go out there.' He was giving rides around the track, and quite a few people gathered on pit road to watch.

"The first time he came in, everybody was laughing and having a good time. The passenger got out of the car, and as he was slipping out of the window, Pearson pulled out a water gun, and he started shooting at the person's crotch area. The person didn't know it; [he was] caught up in the moment. When he got fully out of the car, everybody was kinda laughing at him, thinking he'd wet his pants because he'd scared them. He did it to several people. He couldn't do it succession, because everybody would know.

"It was one of his old tricks. He'd give a track ride, and he'd fill the pistol with water, and let 'em have it unbeknownst to them. Everyone had a good chuckle out of him, including him. They said 'Wait a minute!' when they saw him with that water gun.

"He denied it at first, but then he started laughing and showing everybody that water gun."

Let that be a lesson; bring your own water pistol when you ride with Pearson the prankster. —T.G.

All's Well That Ends Well

Smokey Yunick, perhaps the best mechanic to ever turn a wrench in NASCAR, had his good and bad days at race tracks, but perhaps not many worse than the Southern 500 in 1957. The drivers of Yunick's two Fords, Paul Goldsmith and

Curtis Turner, had qualified first and third, and all through the preliminaries, it looked as if one or the other would be a shoo-in for a victory.

The first thing that went wrong was that Yunick didn't know about a little side bet between the two.

"Our big problem was that Goldy got with a bunch of gamblers and guaranteed them he would not lead the first lap," Yunick told author Peter Golenbock for his book *American Zoom*.

"But Turner got with another bunch of gamblers out of Atlanta and he guaranteed them *he* would not lead the first lap. They come off of Turn 4, Goldy in front trying to slow down to make Turner go by him. They went across the start-finish line the first lap in the race with Goldy on the brakes with all four tires smoking, and Turner pushing him. Cotton Owens led the first lap."

Before 50 miles were in the books, Fonty Flock spun out, and Goldsmith and Bobby Myers hit him. Tragically, Myers was killed, and both Goldsmith and Flock went to the hospital. Then Lee Petty ran into Turner, sending him to the hospital. They fixed Turner's car and put Joe Weatherly at the wheel, but Weatherly could finish no better than 11th.

"That really pissed me off, because the *Saturday Evening Post* was going to give me $25,000 for my life story *if* I won the Darlington race," Yunick said.

Things got completely out of hand when Yunick tried to leave the track. Some guy in a brand new DeSoto inched his way in front of Yunick's new Ford, blocking his way.

"I jumped out of my car and went over to him and said, 'Buddy, that's a damn nice-looking car.'... I said, 'I'm hot and I'm tired. I've got to get to the hospital in a hurry.'"

Yunick said he politely asked the guy to back up, and the guy said, "Screw you."

"A state trooper was standing there looking at the whole thing," Yunick said. "I walked back to the guy in back of me and said, 'Back up a little bit.' He backed up five or six feet. I backed up and put that SOB in low gear, and I flew forward and whapped that DeSoto, and car parts flew everywhere.

"That trooper came over to the other car and he said to him, 'What the hell are you doing pulling up in front of him? Look what you did to his car. Back her up now.' Then the trooper waved me on.

"The trooper said to me, 'I was watching that thing. It was a chicken-shit deal the way he cut you off. I'm glad you whapped him.'" —J.M. (Golenbock, pp. 65)

When the Ragtops Ruled

In the 21st century, convertibles are a novelty on the highway, but there was a time in the middle of the 20th century when they were popular enough to warrant their own series under NASCAR's ever-expanding umbrella.

From 1956 to 1959, and even later at Darlington, NASCAR's Convertible Division was a popular diversion from the hardtop sedans that raced on a regular basis.

"It was the greatest idea NASCAR ever had and would not stay with it. Its timing was off, I suppose," said H. A. "Humpy" Wheeler, the former president of Charlotte Motor Speedway. "I thought they were really neat....It wasn't the same old thing."

Part of the series' appeal, Wheeler said, was that fans were able to see the drivers grimacing as they fought their cars and the other competitors.

"It made the driver look very vulnerable, so therefore the convertible drivers were looked upon as cheating death," Wheeler said. "It added a dimension to it, and really it's silly, because the only difference between them and hardtops was a little piece of sheet metal."

The series was born out of necessity, since NASCAR in the late '50s had tracks clamoring for Grand National (now Sprint Cup) races, and only so many Grand National teams. NASCAR founder Bill France Sr. saw the popularity of the ragtops that were running in the Midwest under the aegis of an organization called SAFE. Soon after, he "merged" NASCAR with SAFE.

The convertible series did have its share of landmark races in its short history: Richard Petty's first race, on July 12, 1958, came in a convertible event at Columbia (South Carolina) Speedway. The first event ever run at Daytona International Speedway was a convertible race on February 20, 1959. And what many old-timers call the greatest race ever run was the battle between upstart Fred Lorenzen and veteran Curtis Turner in the 1961 Rebel 300 at Darlington.

NASCAR discontinued the series after 1959, but France allowed the "zipper tops" (hardtops with removable tops) to run at Darlington because track president Bob Colvin was such a fan of the convertibles.

The drivers, too, loved riding in the breeze.

"I loved racing the convertibles at Darlington," said two-time Grand National champion Ned Jarrett. "Not only could the fans see the drivers, the drivers could see so much better.

"You have to remember, in those days they still had a guard rail (not a concrete wall) and you had to actually bank your car off the rail through the turns to get around the racetrack with any speed at all. Without the top, you could see just where on the rail you needed to hit it, so it was much easier. It was exciting racing."

The late Jim Hunter, who later became president at Darlington, was a student at the University of South Carolina back in 1959 and did not see the first ragtop race at Darlington.

"That day, I was practicing football," Hunter said. "But I listened to it on the radio, and it even *sounded* more exciting!" — J.M.

Follow That Pace Car!

The friendship between Bob Colvin, the second president of Darlington, and driver "Little" Joe Weatherly is evidenced by the fact that Colvin named the museum he built at the track the Joe Weatherly Stock Car Museum.

But Colvin once showed his affection for the pugnacious little Virginian in a more subtle way.

The 1960 Rebel 300 race for NASCAR's Convertible Division cars was halted by rain after 74 laps on May 7, with Fireball Roberts in the lead. It was scheduled to be completed the following Saturday.

Weatherly had led but lost the lead when he pitted before the rains came. NASCAR at first said that the race would be restarted under green-flag conditions, which brought protests from the drivers who had already pitted, since it would, in effect, give the non-pitting drivers a free pit stop.

NASCAR then reversed its decision, saying that the race would be restarted with five laps under the caution flag, giving the cars that hadn't pitted ample time for service.

This is where the Weatherly–Colvin friendship came in.

Colvin asked his buddy to hang around Darlington and help him promote Round 2, and all week long Weatherly could be seen on street corners in Darlington handing out little green flags to passers by.

Colvin did his part. As the driver of the pace car, all week long he'd promised fans "the fastest caution laps ever run." And he delivered.

Fortunately, the race didn't hang in the balance because Roberts was eventually sidelined with mechanical problems, and Weatherly easily won.

The punch line, however, came a few weeks later, when Colvin was traveling through another state, driving the same pace car, and was stopped by a policeman.

The officer accused him of driving 90 mph in a 30-mph zone, and when Colvin protested, the officer said, "This is the Darlington pace car and you drove it 90 mph when you should have driven it 30 mph. You cost Fireball the race and me $25 bucks that I had bet on him. So you can either post a $25 bond or go to jail!"

Colvin paid the fine without a protest. "Hell, I'd have been mad, too, if I'd lost $25," he said. —J.M. (Hunter, pp. 61–63)

Almost Awesome

The first time I met Bill Elliott in person was the spring of 1989 at Darlington. Elliott had broken his wrist in a wreck at Daytona, and I had a question for him.

Being a rookie at NASCAR, I walked right up and tried to talk to him. I didn't know that Winston Cup's most popular driver didn't have many fans in the media and vice versa.

Bill's PR lady asked what they could do for me, and I said I'd like to ask Bill if he felt he could win with the broken wrist.

She said that was a variation of questions Elliott had heard before, but she approached him anyway. Elliott, who always appeared friendly on TV, turned and glared at me. I asked my question, and he half-turned away.

He turned back, made a false start with his standard "Let me put it to you this way…" and then his words came out in a burst.

"If I thought I couldn't win, I wouldn't get in the car," he spat out. "You *always* think you can win."

I took mental notes of our interview for the next few minutes, and Elliott kept up the pace. Finally, he wound down, and his attitude changed. He thanked me for talking to him, and we shook hands. I got my first smile from him, a cross between Huck Finn and Opie.

During the race, Elliott battled and finished sixth. It wasn't awesome enough for Awesome Bill, but it was a pretty good start.

Funny, but I got my best interview with Elliott several years later on the media tour. I started asking questions, and a bunch of TV cameramen came along to tape it. Got some good stuff.
—T.G.

When Racing Was Racin'

Cale Yarborough's stellar career (83 wins, sixth on the all-time list) is intricately tied to Darlington Raceway and, specifically, the Southern 500.

No one was better at winning the fall classic than Yarborough. His five Southern 500 victories were the standard until Jeff Gordon tied it with his fifth win in the race in 2002. The record likely will never be broken—unless, that is, NASCAR has a change of heart and reinstates the tradition of racing on Labor Day weekend in South Carolina instead of in California.

But, according to Yarborough, there are ties and there are ties. Gordon's record at least ought to have an asterisk.

"I think Jeff ought to have to win six to equal my five," Yarborough once said, laughing, "because my first one was on the old track, and it was twice as hard to win."

Modern-day drivers consider Darlington among the toughest—if not *the* toughest—tracks on which they compete, simply because it is so difficult to drive. But Yarborough, who won on the track in 1968 before it was "modernized" by widening it in 1969, said that the before and after versions are entirely different.

In the old days, the exit off of Turn 4—now Turn 2, since the track was flip-flopped in 1997—required a driver to intentionally "kiss" the outside guardrail with his right rear bumper every lap in order to make it through the turn.

Five hundred miles of that, Yarborough said, "was absolutely nerve-wracking. And you had to touch it every lap if you wanted to be fast. The trick was in knowing how hard to hit it not to tear up your car."

In the old days, he said, the "Darlington Stripe" was a badge of honor, since the scuff marks proved a driver was getting everything possible out of his car. Since the reconfiguration, it is a sign a driver had screwed up.

In 2003, before the final Labor Day race at Darlington, Yarborough was invited to take part in a pre-race parade lap in a specially prepared race car as a salute to long-time Winston Cup sponsor R.J. Reynolds Tobacco.

He didn't exactly challenge Gordon to a match race, but well…

"It would be one heck of a last lap, I'll tell you that," Yarborough said. "I can guarantee you I'd be in the victory circle. I might have to bump him up a little bit, but I'd get it done." —J.M.

Building Balmer's Box

Usually, when a race track names a grandstand or other facility after someone it's a measure of respect.

Talladega Superspeedway's Allison Grandstands is named for the first family of the "Alabama Gang." Daytona has grandstands named for Dale Earnhardt, Fireball Roberts, and Richard Petty. Atlanta Motor Speedway has its own Richard Petty and Earnhardt grandstands.

But "Balmer's Box" at Darlington was a not-so-affectionate appellation given the old open-air press box. In fact, it was not named after old-time driver Earl Balmer by the track officials at all, but by the press members in attendance at the 1966 Southern 500.

Earl Balmer, an infrequent competitor on NASCAR's old Grand National circuit during the 1960s, achieved his distinction after he arrived unannounced during the 1966 classic.

At Darlington, the press box was located in Turn 1, which offered reporters an excellent view of the start-finish line, but turned out to be directly in the line of Balmer's fire. On lap 189 of the 364-lap race, Balmer and Richard Petty tangled as their cars entered the turn. Balmer's Dodge rode the guardrail that was only about 15 feet from the press box, spewing debris and gasoline all over the 100 to 125 members of the press.

"We were diving for cover like soldiers seeking the sanctuary of a foxhole," said noted *Charlotte Observer* writer Tom Higgins.

"I thought sure as hell I was going into that press box," Balmer said. "All I could think of was, 'Oh, those poor people up there.'"

No one, including Balmer, was injured in the incident, but the press wrote up a petition before abandoning the box, demanding that track president Bob Colvin find them a safer place to sit.

"I thought I was on fire," said Benny Phillips, the late reporter for the *High Point* (North Carolina) *Enterprise*. "A big piece of wood bounced off my head, and gasoline drenched me. I remember when it was over. I told them I'd beat the hell out of anybody if they lit a cigarette, providing I was still around. Luckily, nobody did."

When the reporters returned the next spring to find a sturdier press facility, they not-so-affectionately called it "Balmer's Box" for many years. —J.M. (Fielden, Vol. III, pp. 101–2, Engel, pp. 86)

chapter 4

A Pair from the Palmetto State

Cale Yarborough holds trophy for winning Pocono 500, 7-30-79

Two of the greatest drivers in NASCAR history came from the Palmetto State of South Carolina—David Pearson from Spartanburg and Cale Yarborough from Timmonsville.

Jim McLaurin, who covered NASCAR throughout his career at The State in that state's capital of Columbia, has heard more than his share of stories about the two of them over the years.

"I Saw That Ocean a Minute Ago..."

Cale Yarborough had the reputation of being the toughest man to ever drive a stock car. Listen, Yarborough was tough before he ever got into big-time racing.

As a youth, Yarborough was bitten by a rattlesnake, hit by lightning, and wrestled an alligator—quite by accident, but wrestled nonetheless.

Before he caught on with a big-time team in racing, he also had a reputation as the world's worst skydiver. Yarborough and one of his daredevil buddies—there seemed to be a plethora of them around his hometown of Timmonsville in the 1950s—put on thrill shows on Sunday afternoons that eventually included jumping out of airplanes.

Skydiving had not reached the degree of sophistication that it has today; indeed, with old Army surplus parachutes, it involved more jump-and-hope than skill. Still, word got out about Yarborough and Harold Lyles' derring-do, and they were hired to jump at the Beaufort Water Festival for the munificent sum of $50 each.

Beaufort is a small town located on the South Carolina coast, and the two were to jump from 10,000 feet and splash land in Port Royal Sound, where they would be picked up by boat.

For the more experienced Lyles, that was no problem. Yarborough had never jumped from that height, nor in such a stiff breeze as was the case that day, and he found himself drifting towards the center of town.

As he got closer, he saw that he was about to hit some power lines, so he lifted his feet. Not enough. He climbed the chute cords. Yarborough barely missed the power lines, but landed, of all places, on top of a dentist's office.

Yarborough was not so embarrassed by having to be rescued by the fire department, nor by landing on the dentist's office.

"I had to be the only skydiver in history who ever missed an ocean," he said. —J.M. (Yarborough, Neely, pp. 117)

"Where's Richard?"

Hall of Fame driver David Pearson may have been the coolest customer to ever drive a race car, but according to the men who raced with him, he had his moments.

In the 1976 Daytona 500, the one in which he and arch-rival Richard Petty tangled on the last lap, Pearson's calm demeanor cracked, if only briefly.

Eddie Wood, who now is a part-owner of the famous Wood Brothers team for which Pearson drove, was just another crew guy in that race.

"I was on the radio with him when he crashed with Petty," Wood recalled during a visit to the team's Stuart, Virginia, shop in 2000. Pearson didn't say a word until the pair came out of the second turn, and then he only said, "I'm gonna try him here," Wood said. When they got to turn 3, Pearson said, "I got him."

That triumph was short-lived, because Petty made his charge on the inside as they came through 3 and 4. And all hell broke loose. In those days, crews did not have TV monitors, so they were at the mercy of the crowd reaction and whatever their driver told them over the radio.

"The bitch hit me," according to Wood, was all that Pearson said.

But the "Silver Fox" quickly regained his composure: "At this time, he's spinning backwards headed toward the infield and says, 'Where's Richard?' just as calm as he could be," Wood said. "'Where's Richard?' And I said, "He's up here. He's stopped." And David says, "Well I'm coming."

The old films show Pearson's No. 21 Mercury limping across the grass and just making it back on the racetrack to take the checkered flag in one of the most exciting finishes in racing history.

At this point in the story, Len Wood, who was also on the sidelines that day, put in his two cents: "I'd just like to say something about that," he said. "Somebody comes up to Pearson after the race and says, 'Was you mad?' Pearson said, 'No, but I was getting ready to be if I hadn't won that race.'" —J.M.

Turtle, Tiny, and Cale

There was perhaps no odder couple in racing than when Herman "the Turtle" Beam asked Cale Yarborough to be his driver in the early 1960s.

Beam never won a race in NASCAR's top division but nonetheless held the record for consecutive finishes (84) simply because he went slow and stayed out of everybody else's way. Yarborough, on the other hand, was a disciple of Junior Johnson's philosophy: "All I want back is the steering wheel."

According to Yarborough, Beam wanted to win races, but he wanted to keep the car looking showroom new, too.

"I kept telling him that the two thoughts didn't go together," Yarborough said. "It's like telling someone they can go swimming if they don't get wet."

Neither man, however, could have anticipated what happened in the Nashville 400. Throughout the race, Beam kept flashing the message "E-Z" on Yarborough's pit board, which Yarborough of course ignored.

When the engine in Tiny Lund's Ford blew on lap 194, initiating a huge crash, Yarborough managed to miss the wreck, but not the man. Lund's car caught fire, and the 6'5", 270-pound driver leaped from his car and ran blindly across the track.

"He wanted to get away from it as fast as he could—before it blew up, I guess," Yarborough said. "He didn't see me coming down the track, and ran square into my right hand door. It didn't hurt Tiny, but it bent the whole door in."

Later, Beam told his driver: "You see there? If you'd have slowed down, he'd have missed you!" —J.M. (Yarborough, Neely, pp. 130, Fielden, Vol. II, pp. 219)

Cale and Jaws

Cale Yarborough and Darrell Waltrip, two racing giants, were not best buddies. Not even close.

"He was always running his mouth, and he was always eating up race cars," Cale has said. "So I nicknamed him 'Jaws' because he was always flapping his jaws. I respected him as a driver, but I wasn't going to let him run over me, too."

In the 1982 Gabriel 400 at Michigan, Yarborough and Waltrip were battling back and forth for the lead, and, finally,

Cale won and slowed as he took the checkered flag. DW floored it, heading straight for Yarborough. In a classic wrestling move, Cale swerved, and Darrell whiffed and sailed into the infield mud.

One assumes that Yarborough was grinning ear-to-ear as a tow truck pulled Waltrip's car out of the muck.

But Waltrip got the last laugh. It probably still galls Cale that Darrell wound up with 84 wins to Yarborough's 83, leaving DW tied with Bobby Allison for fourth on the all-time NASCAR Sprint Cup Series victory list.

Waltrip once told me that he and Yarborough weren't bitter rivals, though; in fact, he said that when Cale was about to leave Junior Johnson's team, he called DW over and suggested he ask Johnson about the ride. Waltrip did, posted two 12-win seasons, and won three Cup titles (1981, '82, and '85) with Junior.

Waltrip says he had only two major worries while working for Junior.

"[When] we went to a racetrack," DW said, "we worried about where we'd pit and where was victory circle. That was all we worried about. And how big was the trophy so we'd be sure to have enough room to carry it home."

Thanks for the assist, Cale. —T.G.

David Pearson, Meet Faron Young

At the peak of David Pearson's splendid driving career, he picked up the nickname "Silver Fox" because he drove as much with his head as his right foot.

Pearson had a reputation for letting the hotheads wear out their equipment early in the race while he coddled his along and saved it for when it counted. But even Pearson had to learn those lessons the hard way.

In his early years, he was one of the hardest chargers on the track, and that was nowhere more evident than in Atlanta in 1961, the season after Pearson won rookie of the year honors.

Pearson got in a big tangle early in the summer race and watched most of it from the sidelines. "You might say I learned a lesson that day," Pearson said later. "That was the first time I hit the wall hard on a superspeedway. I was sore for a week."

It was at about the same time that country and western singer Faron Young's smash hit—no pun intended—"Hello Walls" hit the charts, and the folks in Pearson's hometown of Spartanburg, South Carolina, drove the lesson home.

"All I heard on the radio for a week was the song, 'Hello, Walls.' This disc jockey in Spartanburg must have dedicated that song to me at least 15 times a day. Everywhere I went, people in town were asking me if I'd heard my song today. My song, they called it.

"Every time I hear that song now, it reminds me of hitting the wall." —J.M. (Hunter, pp. 80)

Excuse Me, Ma'am, Could I Borrow a Towel?

Before race car drivers owned their own private jets and stayed in their luxurious motorhomes at racetracks, they often traveled together and, on occasion, bunked together to cut expenses.

One pair that frequently buddied up was the Mutt and Jeff combination of Tiny Lund and Cale Yarborough. Before they could afford even a motel room, the 6'5" Lund and 5'9" Yarborough often slept on a mattress in the back of Lund's Pontiac station wagon.

It made for fast friends and sometimes outrageous pranks.

Once, Yarborough and Lund were staying at a motel and roughhousing in the pool after a hard day at the racetrack. Lund maneuvered Yarborough out into the deep end, where he still had solid footing and Yarborough didn't, and kept dunking the smaller driver.

Yarborough put up with it, but plotted his revenge.

When Lund went in to take a shower, Yarborough took the trash can from the room, went out to the ice machine, and loaded it up. Then he filled it with water and stirred for several minutes to achieve maximum effect, then snuck back into the room and dumped it over the top of the shower door onto Lund.

Lund, of course, bolted out of the shower and took off after Yarborough. The chase went around and around the motel parking lot until Lund, naked as a jaybird, ran smack into the proverbial little old lady, who was just getting out of her car.

According to Yarborough, she looked directly into Lund's belly button.

" ' 'Scuse me, ma'am,'" he said and dashed back to his room.

Yarborough, meanwhile, watched the scene with more than a little amusement.

"The last time I saw her, she was standing there, motionless, with one hand on the car door and the other over her eyes," he said. —J.M. (Yarborough, Neely, pp. 131)

Let Me Show You How It's Done

David Pearson was not always the sly old "Silver Fox," popping up out of the weeds to win races that he looked completely out of.

Everett "Cotton" Owens, who was also from Spartanburg, South Carolina, was more noted as a car owner but was a pretty fair driver himself. He won hundreds of NASCAR modified races, and he had nine Grand National wins to his credit.

Owens had long since hung up his driving helmet when he hired Pearson in the early 1960s, but it didn't take Owens long to figure out he needed to teach him a thing or two about driving.

In 1964, he came out of retirement for one race to do it.

"It was a situation where David was young and wasn't listening to what we had to say to him," Owens said. "He'd come in the pits so wild that it would run the crew completely back over the wall, and he was losing about 15 to 20 seconds on a pit stop.

"I told him one day, 'Pearson, there's gonna come a day when I'm gonna show you I can beat you because you won't listen.'"

That opportunity came at Richmond, Virginia. Owens wound up with one more car than he had drivers for, and he didn't waste any time. Despite making his qualifying run late in the session, a definite disadvantage in those days, Owens qualified third-fastest. Pearson, along with another young colt named Richard Petty, was well back in the pack.

"They hollered up at me and told me, 'You've been out of racing so long you don't even know where the drivers' meeting is." I stepped it off back down there and told them that I wanted them to notice how many paces I was ahead of them already. I went on and won the race, and it liked to have killed them."

Pearson did not take the loss well.

"He thought the crew had turned against him or something or another—they didn't do it right," Owens said. "It was all a part of the learning process. It's hard for a rookie coming in now to know all the secrets of getting into the pits and getting a good, quick pit stop without losing too many positions. That happened even back then.

"He was sort of upset, but he began to listen to us and he began to win races instead of giving them away."

Not that Pearson stayed young and wild. By the time Pearson finished his career with 105 victories, Owens said he'd learned a thing or two.

"Believe me, I have seen a lot of great drivers, but I have never seen a driver who could out-drive David Pearson," he said. "He could go anywhere, anytime, and [he] could sit up front on a race track he'd never seen before. He just had that natural driving ability."

His old boss wasn't half-bad, either. —J.M.

chapter 5
The Fabulous Baker Boys

Richard Petty (left),
Buddy Baker (center)
at Winston 500 at
Talladega, 5-5-72

When NASCAR named its 50 greatest drivers
as it celebrated its 50th anniversary,
Buck and Buddy Baker both made the list.

At a ceremony in Daytona, each driver was
introduced and given a snazzy leather jacket for
being selected. They sat down in rows of chairs
while the rest of the group was introduced.

The Bakers, coming as high in the alphabet
as they did, had a long time to sit there.
All of the drivers had put their jackets on,
but Buck Baker was holding his in his lap.
Buddy was trying to tell his father to
put it on, but Buck wasn't having it.
And Buddy just laughed about it.

That summed up their personalities perfectly.

No Punches Pulled

The late Elzie Wylie "Buck" Baker, the first man to win two consecutive NASCAR Grand National championships, was a hero of NASCAR's rough-and-tumble days, and he had a knack for storytelling that nearly matched his driving skills.

At the end of Baker's driving career, he operated a successful driving school at North Carolina Motor Speedway in Rockingham and, in 1998, sat down and told a couple of tales out of school.

Asked who his brightest pupils at the school were, Baker said, "I guess you know who I'm going to say. Jeff Gordon and the Burton brothers [Jeff and Ward] were about the best; they're the ones I bring out first. You talk about the guys who have been successful.

"To tell you the truth, I didn't see an awful lot in Jeff Gordon until he got settled in there. He came to the school and his mother had to rent his car for him. He could buy the company now, couldn't he?"

Even his own family was fair game.

When asked about his son Buddy, he pulled no punches.

"When he first started out, he could tear up a damn anvil," Buck said. "He works with me in the school, occasionally. The only thing about Buddy is, he hates for me to get hold of the microphone.

"We had a bunch of executives down there and I got up and told them they were the no-drivingest people I'd ever seen in my life. Buddy was trying to take the mic from me the whole time. I think they came to like it. That happened on Friday, and they were kidding with me by the time they got ready to leave.

"There wasn't a one of them that could change gears in a four-speed transmission. I told a guy I thought I'd put automatic transmissions in 'em. A lot of the students say, 'Oh, yeah, we can drive a four-speed,' until you get 'em in there.

"When you buy a clutch two or three times a class, that gets old, you know?" —J.M.

BOOP! The Fickle Finger of Fate

Buddy Baker, a Hall of Fame driver and talker, says the funniest thing he ever saw in a race happened at 11:00 in the evening, when he was running the 24-hour race at Daytona. He was an innocent bystander.

Baker and the guy in front of him were driving powerful Porsches. As the lead Porsche cut through the infield road course, a tiny car got over into him, tearing up the side of the Porsche.

The Porsche driver, going much faster than his assailant, slammed his brakes as Baker's lights lit the scene.

"This guy driving the Porsche rolls the window down, wearing DayGlo driving gloves, and he shoots the bird at this guy!" said Baker, nearly rolling off his chair. "He slowed up to give him the bird, to make sure he could see it."

In other words, a bright middle finger blazed in the dark.

"He gave this guy the bird and then vanished off into the dark. I almost wrecked laughing. It was too funny to put to words. I saw that big driving glove come out, and the bird came up, boop! With that DayGlo driving glove, that hand looked six-foot tall when he stuck it out there."

Buddy couldn't remember how he did in the race, but he remembered the glove. —T.G.

No Fooling Around

Buddy Baker was on his way to winning the 1970 Southern 500 at Darlington Raceway, driving then for legendary car owner Cotton Owens.

"On the white-flag lap, with nothing to gain at all, I came off Turn 4 and got way sideways," Baker says. "But I made the lap, won the race, and pulled into the winner's circle."

Owens was already there.

"Cotton looked at me and said, 'I am going to tell you something,'" Baker said. "'If you had wrecked that car on the white-flag lap, if the wreck didn't kill you, I would have.'" —D.P.

Faster Than Fast

Buddy Baker won the first Busch Clash in 1979 and the Daytona 500 in 1980. He won four times at Charlotte and four times at Talladega. He also was the first driver to break the 200-mph barrier on a superspeedway, running 200.447 mph in a 1969 Dodge Daytona on March 24, 1970, at Talladega.

"I went down there for a transmission test," Baker said. "We were trying to work out a good transmission for restarts. The first lap we ran was 199.9 mph and we all said, 'Wait a minute, we may have some history here!'"

NASCAR was paid to bring in the official clocks, and Baker broke the 200-mph barrier.

"I said, 'Let's slick it up and really give them a good lap,'" Baker said. "The car would do 215; it was that good. They said I had done what I had to do. There was the 100-mph mark, then the 200-mph mark. They said, 'If you think you can run 300, we'll fix it up.' I said, 'We'd better not go there.'"

Baker was at his best on the big tracks, where he could feed his need for speed.

"The perfect driver," he joked. "A size 2 hat and a size 14 shoe."

Baker doesn't mind making himself the butt of his humor.

"The car I won the Daytona 500 in?" Baker asked. "I've often said Ray Charles could have run third in it with curb feelers on the right side. It was a pretty good car."

There's a great story there, too.

By the time Baker won the Daytona 500 in 1980, he was known to joke that he'd won the Daytona 475 three or four times but something odd had always happened to deny him the victory. Finally, he got the job done in that great car and he'd won the sport's biggest race.

"I got back to the room that night and tried to go to sleep," Baker says. "About the time I'd be just about to doze off, I'd wake up and say to myself, 'I won the Daytona 500!'"

Baker knew he wasn't going to sleep, so he decided to get up, put his stuff in the car, and make another 500-mile drive back to his home in Charlotte.

"I had just crossed the state line from Florida into Georgia," Baker says. "And I was really hauling it. I went by this state patrolman and I knew he had me. I just pulled over and waited on him."

The trooper walked up to Baker's car and recognized its driver.

"He walked up to the car and said, 'Buddy Baker, I'll declare,'" Baker says. "'I've followed your career for a long time, and you just have never had any luck. And tonight is another example of that.'" —D.P.

The Stretcher Story

Unquestionably, the all-time Buddy Baker story comes from 1967 and a race at a track in Maryville, Tennessee. Baker won the pole and knew he had a strong race car that night. He was leading by a bunch when he felt a little something funny.

"I went down into Turn 3 and I felt this little rumble," Baker said. "I thought a wheel weight had come off or something. I went down the front straightaway, and when I turned it went 'Boom!'"

His tire blew, and Baker's car went headfirst into the wall. Baker was dazed, perhaps even knocked out for a bit, and the next thing he knew an ambulance was pulling alongside his car. To this day, Baker calls the two men who got out "Bubba and Barney Fife," and they began by trying to pull Baker out of the car—headfirst—without unhooking his safety harness.

They finally helped Baker, who had broken ribs, onto a stretcher that had wheels on it and loaded him into the back of the ambulance. They forgot, however, to lock the wheels down or secure the back door. So as the ambulance tried to go up the high-banked track to take Baker out and to the hospital, the stretcher rolled into the door and the door flew open— dumping Baker onto the track.

"I'm on the gurney with my arms and legs strapped down and these cars are coming at me," Baker said. The race had not been stopped, cars were still running under caution. "I got one arm out and started waving my hand at them a little."

The cars dodged Baker, but that didn't stop the rolling gurney. Baker was still rolling down the banking, and when he rolled off the pavement the gurney's wheels dug into the mud and flipped Baker—still strapped to the stretcher—face first into the mud.

"One of the guys from the ambulance jumped out, grabbed me and rolled me over," Baker said. "He said, 'Are you OK?'

"I said, 'If I ever get off this thing, I am going to kill you.'" —D.P.

A Tiny Bear for Buddy

Years after Tiny Lund's death in 1975, Buddy Baker always has a Tiny story at the ready. He once talked about a post-race incident as Lund raised dust as he stalked toward Buddy. The men had just bumped fenders and bumpers on track, and Lund apparently wanted to dent Baker's nose.

"I looked up and said, 'Oh, Lord,'" Baker said with a laugh. "Tiny was racing me, and I was racing to win. I tried to get around him four or five times, so I just moved him. It kinda made him mad."

Naturally. Baker says he noticed part of an axle about the length of a ball bat.

"My first thought," he has said, "was to take the axle and whop him across the head. Then it occurred to me, 'What if I miss?'"

So how did Baker handle the aroused and not-so-tiny DeWayne Lund?

"I was a good salesman, and I had a boost of adrenaline," Baker told me, laughing. "I said, 'You, of all people, are upset at me? You hit me four or five times in one corner!' He turned around laughing and walked off. I thought, 'Are you kidding me?'"

Baker, who was also 6'6" but not as hefty as Lund, was asked if he was happy that the outsized Tiny departed without hostilities.

"You tell me, if you were in a river and a bear got in, would you be happy when it went away?"

Absolutely. Especially a Tiny bear. —T.G. (*Hickory Record*)

chapter 6

The Legend of Ingle Hollow

Junior Johnson, Atlanta, 6-3-64 before Dixie Stock Car Race

Junior Johnson is a legend so many
times over it's almost not fair.

He's one of the best drivers in NASCAR's
history. Few people could do more
building and working on cars.
Few car owners had anywhere near
as much success as Johnson had.

Beyond all of that, he might be one of the
most colorful characters who has ever lived,
in or out of stock car racing.

Pop Goes the Windshield

The biggest win of Junior Johnson's driving career was a slapped-together, against-all-odds deal that was so wildly improbable that Hollywood would have never touched it. If the script writers had, however, the title would have had to have been "Gone With the Wind."

For starters, Johnson had not planned to enter the Daytona 500 because he did not have a ride. Then he was approached by car builder/owner Ray Fox with a deal. John Mansoni owned the Daytona Beach Kennel Club, the dog-racing track located just outside the year-old Daytona International Speedway, and he wanted a car in the race, cost be damned.

Mansoni, in fact, offered Fox double the going rate to build a car. Fox had a 1959 Chevrolet that could be turned into a race car, but the problem was, he had only eight days to do it, and he had no driver—until he talked Johnson into coming on board.

This was many years before race teams were large and sophisticated enough to turn out assembly-line cars, but with a handful of helpers, they got it done.

Johnson had his misgivings because the Chevrolets in that era were woefully underpowered, particularly next to the big Pontiacs, and he didn't want to go to the race just to ride around.

When he began practice, however, he discovered something that no one else had. When he was passed by a Pontiac, he found that if he could latch onto its tail, he could stay right with the faster car despite his Chevy's lack of power.

Johnson didn't know it, but he'd discovered the "bloody black art" of drafting.

"I wanted to be sure of what I'd hit on, so I went back out to practice alone," Johnson said. "The car was still the same—pretty slow." But when he found a Pontiac, "They couldn't shake me," he said. "I knew then I was right about the air creating a situation—a slipstream type of thing—in which a slower car could keep up with a much faster one. I saw this gave me a chance to win the race."

That being said, it still required a huge dose of luck.

The race was such a crash-filled melee, however, that only 39 of the original field of 68 cars finished. Most of the top Pontiacs were gone due to one circumstance or other, and Johnson found himself racing Tommy Johns' Pontiac for the win.

Johns breezed by Johnson on lap 170 of 200 and appeared headed for the win. But then, on lap 192, something curious happened.

"One of the damnedest things I ever saw on a race track," Johnson said. "The back glass popped out of Bobby's car and flew into the air. I think our speed and the traffic circumstances combined to create a vacuum that sucked that back glass right out."

The sudden change in airflow caused Johns to spin out. He did not crash, but by the time he got headed in the right direction, Johnson said, "I was long gone."

And on his way to victory. —J.M. (Higgins, Waid, pp. 48–49)

Fast Is a Relative Term

To say that NASCAR founder Bill France made racing a new game when he completed his monstrous, 2.5-mile track called Daytona International Speedway is something of an understatement.

For a bunch of guys who had cut their racing teeth on the little half-mile dirt "bull rings" that dotted the Southeast, the only "big track" they'd ever seen was the one at Darlington, and it was only 1⅓ miles around.

Daytona was a whole 'nother smoke.

Fireball Roberts' pole-winning speed at Darlington for the Southern 500 in 1959 was 123.734 mph. Cotton Owens' pole speed for the first Daytona 500, in 1959, was 143.198.

Owens' pole win at Daytona the following February was 149.892 mph, and Fireball Roberts set the top speed in qualifying at 151.556. Considering that the top speeds at most short tracks were nearly 50 mph slower than that, Daytona must have felt more like a launch pad than a race track.

In the inaugural race in 1959, only 31 of the field of 59 cars were running at the checkered flag, and in 1960, 30 of the field of 68 were in the garage at the finish, and most of the ones sidelined were due to crashes. Some said that the problem was the fact that most of the drivers were unaccustomed to the high speeds.

But there was at least one it didn't bother.

Junior Johnson, who won that Daytona 500 in 1960, said that he'd gone faster on the back roads of North Carolina when he was hauling moonshine.

"I guess that's probably the reason a lot of 'em wrecked, but the speed wasn't a problem to me," Johnson said. "See, my liquor-hauling cars were light and they had big engines.… So in running a race car at Daytona, it's not like I was sitting down in something I wasn't used to.

"We were going about 150 mph at Daytona. I had run cars faster than that on the highway," he said. "I had run 'em so fast on the highway sometimes that the road ahead looked only about a foot wide." —J.M. (Higgins, Waid, pp. 49, 51)

Right on the Money

Junior Johnson grew up in Wilkes County, North Carolina, and has always lived there. He was, of course, the local at North Wilkesboro Speedway, but even he underestimated the strength of his support.

Johnson had just come back from "working for the government"—the local bootleggers' euphemism for spending some time behind bars for making moonshine—when he found himself engaged in a hot and heavy battle for a win at his home track.

During the race, something happened between Johnson and his rival that apparently did not set well with someone in the grandstands, and the guy heaved an object onto the track.

Track promoter Enoch Staley remembered it this way: "I saw something sail out of the stands and over the fence, right in front of [Johnson's opponent's] car. It hit the track and broke into a thousand pieces. It was a quart-sized fruit jar filled with white liquor.

"We were strong against anything being thrown on the track, but this was sort of amusing because of what the object happened to be. I couldn't imagine a man getting so mad he'd throw away a quart of good moonshine."

Once he'd avoided the shattered glass, Johnson watched what came next with amusement.

"I saw that the law had come to the scene and was trying to arrest the guy," he said. "There was a pretty lively scuffle going on 'til the deputies got him handcuffed and took him off."

But that, according to Staley, wasn't the funny part.

"Junior didn't tell the rest of the story," he said. "The fan that got taken to jail was a feller named Ernest Money. He was Junior's uncle." —J.M. (Higgins, Waid, pp. 40)

Just the Good Ol' Boys...

It sounds like something more out of the *Dukes of Hazzard*, but Junior Johnson told it for the truth.

In the 1950s Johnson made more money hauling moonshine than he did on the racetrack, but once he made a haul that included something more than white lightning—free of charge.

It seems that Johnson and his friend Gwyn Staley were both loaded for a run to Lenoir, North Carolina. As they crossed the county line, Johnson noticed some dirt that had been kicked up in the road, so they stopped to investigate.

Out in the bushes, they discovered a car turned up on its side. It turned out that a couple of locals had been sampling some "Wilkes County Champagne" and had run off the road.

"We knew both of the guys in the car," Johnson said. "One of them was the high sheriff. They couldn't hardly stand up."

Neither man was badly hurt, but they couldn't be left where they were, so Johnson and Staley played Good Samaritan.

Each of them squeezed a man in on top of the cases of liquor in their cars, drove into town, and dropped them off—of all places—at the county courthouse. Then they went on their merry way.

"Every once in a while after that," Johnson said, "every time I'd see that sheriff, he'd kinda grin and say, 'You ain't been up the road lately, have you?'" —J.M. (Higgins, Waid, pp. 29)

The Chicken and the Pig

Junior Johnson never won a championship in NASCAR's top series as a driver. That's because he didn't run all of the races. He ran the ones he thought he could win and the ones that paid the most money.

William H. G. France, NASCAR's founder and president through its formative era, tried like the dickens to get Johnson to run a full schedule and race for a championship. At one point, France told Johnson that he needed to be committed to being a racer.

"I thought to myself, 'I am not committed to racing. I'm a bootlegger,'" said Johnson, who did, indeed, serve time in federal prison for bootlegging before getting a presidential pardon for his offense.

So Johnson came up with an analogy to make France understand his level of "commitment" to racing.

"I told him I wasn't committed, I was just involved," Johnson said. "It's like a chicken and a pig. If you're eating bacon and eggs for breakfast, the chicken is involved, but that pig is committed." —D.P.

"And Don't Let the Door Hit You..."

There's no telling how many races Junior Johnson and Bobby Allison might have won if both men had not been so hardheaded, but their short-lived run together ended just for that reason.

Richard Howard, the man who helped pull Charlotte Motor Speedway out of bankruptcy, called on Johnson in 1970 to get him to build a Chevrolet that would put the GM nameplate back at the top of NASCAR racing.

They succeeded while running a partial schedule, but in 1972, they wanted to go full throttle. To do that, they needed a couple of things: a good driver and a sponsor. In Bobby Allison, they found both. Allison had hooked up with Coca-Cola while driving for the noted Holman Moody team, but that organization folded at the end of the 1971 season.

Perfect match?

Not exactly. Both Johnson and Allison had their own ideas about how race cars should be built, and they didn't set horses from the outset. Depending on which man you ask, by midseason they weren't even speaking to each other.

Further exacerbating the situation was the fact that Allison planned to join Ralph Moody in 1973 when he formed his own team, and Johnson knew it. Add to that the fact that Johnson had a young driver named Cale Yarborough champing at the bit to get in one of his cars.

Matters came to a head at Talladega, when Allison's car started smoking due to a dripping oil line. Johnson's crew took only a few laps to repair the damage, but when they went looking for their driver, he'd already left the track.

The straw that broke the camel's back came after the season, when Allison was driving in a Trans-Am race in California. He received a 5:00 AM phone call from Howard wanting to know, in Allison's words, "Are you going to drive for us next year? If you're not, we have a chance to get the best driver in NASCAR."

"Get him," Allison reportedly said and hung up.

Johnson wouldn't confirm or deny that conversation, but noted that he'd made his mind up much earlier. According to him, Howard and Allison were talking at Rockingham that fall, trying to work something out for 1973. Allison said he'd drive, but he wanted all the sponsorship money and half of his winnings. After Talladega, Johnson had heard enough.

"I said, 'Well, he can have all the sponsorship and half the winnings. All he's got to do now is find a damn car to drive.'"
—J.M. (Higgins, Waid, pp. 92, 99–101)

Junior's "Sweet Potato" Rods

R.J. Reynolds Tobacco Company (RJR) sponsored NASCAR's top series for more than three decades, and the company's marketing efforts contributed greatly to the popularity the sport enjoys today.

One of the best things RJR came up with was the circuit's all-star race, now known as the Nextel All-Star Challenge. When it began in 1985, it was called The Winston.

In that first year, the prize for finishing first in the event was $200,000. Later it paid $1 million, but in 1985 no single race on the Winston Cup circuit—not even the Daytona 500—paid $200,000 for the win.

"This," Darrell Waltrip said, "was a big deal."

Waltrip's car owner was Junior Johnson, and Johnson was determined to win the event.

"When Junior put his mind to something you could not stop him," Waltrip said. "He would get after something with the gusto of a hungry hound. We were going to win The Winston, we were going to do whatever it takes."

One day, Waltrip went to the team's shop in Wilkes County, North Carolina, and saw Johnson himself working on something. Johnson told him it was a set of "special" rods for the motor the team would use in the all-star event.

"He called them 'sweet potato rods,'" Waltrip said. "I didn't ask him what that meant."

Johnson said it meant that they were "light and slick." He also told Waltrip that they'd be good for about 165 miles. The all-star race itself was scheduled for 150 miles, so that didn't leave much time for practice or anything else.

Waltrip, of course, won the inaugural running of The Winston.

"I passed Harry Gant on the last lap going into Turn 1 and took the lead down the back straight," Waltrip said. "I was whooping and hollering because I was one happy dude. Coming off Turn 4, if I hadn't had my seatbelt on I would have jumped out of the car. I had my hand out the window waving to the fans and about that time the motor blew all to pieces. Parts went flying for days."

Up in the broadcast booth, Mike Joy was calling the race and Neil Bonnett, who was Waltrip's teammate but was not qualified to run in the winners-only event, was working with him. Joy said that as soon as Waltrip's engine blew up, just as he crossed the finish line to win, Bonnett started hollering.

"Neil said, 'He clutched it! He clutched it!'" Joy said. "Neil was convinced Darrell had blown the engine on purpose."

He wasn't by himself. Ever since that day, Waltrip has had to listen to people accuse him of blowing up the engine so that it couldn't be inspected. Waltrip has tried to brush that aside. "The engine blew up, but it didn't disappear," he's said.

Johnson, on the other hand, is significantly more coy about what was under the hood of that car.

"They claim they checked it; they said it was legal," he said. "But I don't know what they checked."

Johnson, in fact, retired from the sport with a clear reputation for being among the most "creative" in history when it came to building cars and engines that were very close to the "edges" of the rule book.

Johnson is unrepentant.

"If you sharpen a knife, you want the sharpest edge you can get on it," he said. "That's what I did. Whenever we did something, NASCAR might get one thing but I'd keep one. I had two every time I had one. NASCAR got some of it, but they didn't get it all." —D.P.

A Language Barrier

The first time Darrell Waltrip went to Junior Johnson's shop in Wilkes County, the driver was excited and wanted to make a good impression.

"He had coon dogs in the office and race cars in his yard," Waltrip remembers. "I go in his office and there are a couple of dogs on the couch and I said, 'Is there something I can do?'"

Johnson didn't know what to do with his eager driver. But he decided to try to find him something to occupy his time.

"Junior said, 'Go out there and bounce them tires,'" Waltrip said. "Back in those days, to seat the tires on the wheel, you would take the tires and bounce them so the tire would go out against the wheel and not leak. We didn't have tubes.

"There were like 40 tires there. I didn't know how to do it, but I'd seen guys do it. So I bounced a tire and it rolled off down the hill. Another one bounced off a guy's car. I had tires everywhere."

Johnson saw what has happening.

"He [came] out of the door and said, 'Boy, what are you doing?' I said, 'I am bouncing the tires like you told me.'"

Johnson was disgusted.

"He said, 'Get them tires gathered up and get over there on the machine and get them tires bounced like I told you,'" Waltrip said.

What Johnson was actually telling Waltrip to do was "balance" the tires.

"I knew right then we were going to have a communication problem," Waltrip said. —D.P.

Take One for the Team

These days, multicar teams rule the competition in the Nextel Cup Series. With some teams spending $15 million or more just to get one competitive car on the track, having two, three, or even more teams with sponsors helping pay the bills makes it possible for the big teams to marshal all of their resources toward victory.

It has not always been that way.

There have been great multicar operations at various points in NASCAR's history.

Carl Kiekhaefer, who made his fortune in boat engines, had the Flock brothers—Tim, Fonty, and Bob—as well as Buck Baker, Speedy Thompson, and Herb Thomas all driving for him in 1955 and 1956 as his team dominated the sport. In the 1960s John Holman and Ralph Moody fielded factory-backed Fords for some of the sport's top drivers and racked up victory after victory. Richard Petty and Buddy Baker were teammates at Petty Enterprises for a while in the 1970s.

But to varying degrees, the weight of success eventually brought all of those teams down. As Robert Yates once said to Dale Jarrett when he was considering the idea of having more than one team, "The problem with having two cars is they only let you pull one car into victory lane."

If anybody was going to be able to make two teams work, it was going to be Junior Johnson, who'd already proved to the drivers he had hired that he was a master at motivation.

Darrell Waltrip joined Johnson's team in 1981, following Cale Yarborough as driver of the No. 11 Chevrolets. Yarborough had won championships in 1976, 1977, and 1978. Waltrip remembers one contract negotiating session with Johnson near the end of the 1980 season.

"I had my lawyer and Junior had his," Waltrip said. "Junior's guy was about 80 years old, and I had these guys from Connecticut who were really slick. I'd had a contract with 40 pages of all of these 'heretofores' and 'thereafters' and 'in lieu ofs,' and there was no way I was going to get out of it. But they got me out of it.

"So we're in North Wilkesboro in this little room off the side of the courthouse. Junior's lawyer is off in another little room typing up the contract and it's peck, peck, peck. It takes, like, 15 minutes to make a change. We get down the end, and it's one page. My guy was pretty slick and he thought we had a couple of bumpkins we could put something over on."

Waltrip's lawyer looked at Johnson and asked, "Junior, what are you going to do for Darrell if he wins the championship?"

Waltrip remembers what happened next.

"Junior looked down over these little half-glasses he had on," Waltrip said. "He said, 'I can tell you what I am going to do to him if he don't!'"

During races in 1981, when Waltrip did win the championship, by the way, Johnson would get on the radio and urge Waltrip to drive hard. When that didn't work, Johnson would pretend to forget who was in the car.

"He'd call me 'Cale,'" Waltrip said. Yarborough and Waltrip had long been fierce rivals—it was Yarborough who gave Waltrip the nickname "Jaws."

In 1984 Johnson started a second team with Neil Bonnett driving. The teams each had shops near Johnson's home in Wilkes County, North Carolina, divided on the property by a creek. There was a little footbridge across the creek, and Johnson was just about the only guy who ever used it.

"He'd come over to our shop and say, 'Man, you won't believe the horsepower the boys over there across the creek are getting out of their engines,'" Waltrip said. "And our guys would go to work trying to get more horsepower out of our motors. He kept them racing each other harder than they raced anybody else."

Waltrip tried to get Johnson back after he'd left to join another multicar team at Hendrick Motorsports. Waltrip had been telling Johnson that Waddell Wilson was building engines with more power, and when Waltrip went to the Hendrick team, he started working with Wilson.

"Somebody asked me what the difference was," Waltrip said. "I said, 'It's like getting off a mule and getting on a thoroughbred.'"

Reporters went to Johnson to see what Johnson would say about that remark.

"I don't know anything about a thoroughbred," Johnson said, "but I did have a jackass that drove for me last year."
—D.P.

chapter 7
Strange Days Indeed

Bobby Allison

Sometimes, stuff happens for which there is no explanation...or that needs no explanation. You just have to shake your heads, move on, and remember the details for when you tell the story later.

Vroom with a View

As far as things have come in NASCAR over its more than 50 years, one thing that hasn't changed is that the only way to get a race car to a track is to haul it there.

These days, of course, the transporters that haul a team's primary and back-up cars costs upward of $250,000 and carries two cars as well as enough tools and parts to keep them on the track. It also has thousands of dollars worth of equipment teams use to make sure their cars are race-ready and serves as a team's headquarters at the track as well.

In the old days, things weren't quite so elaborate. Even the top-tier teams, like Petty Enterprises and the Wood Brothers, had flat-bed trailers that they towed behind pick-up trucks to tracks as far away as Riverside, California.

In the 1960s on one of those cross-country hauls, the Wood Brothers team had traveled from their headquarters in Stuart, Virginia, to a race at Riverside and were on their way back east when they stopped to eat. After getting back on the road, they heard a roar but couldn't figure out where it was coming from. When they pulled over, however, they figured out that it was coming from their race car on the back of their flat bed.

Sitting in the cockpit was a fan, who'd obviously been "overserved" with libations at the restaurant. The fan had the driver's helmet on and had the accelerator to the floor while turning the steering wheel. He'd climbed into the car and didn't get out before the truck took off, so he decided to make the best of it. —D.P.

Turner, Wingtips, and Tires

Joe Weatherly, Buddy Baker, and Curtis Turner were funny for various reasons. Of course, Weatherly and Baker were *trying* to be funny.

"Curtis Turner was funny...and didn't mean to be," said Humpy Wheeler, once the president and promoter for Charlotte Motor Speedway. "You do that by wearing brown silk suits to Columbia [South Carolina] Speedway with brown, wing-tipped shoes. And he actually took his coat and tie off and drove in the damned thing because he got there too late. He was driving for Junior Johnson."

And he did pretty well. Turner started four times at Columbia, and in his last try there he started second and finished third.

Wheeler also recalled going with a friend to Turner's hospital room when he was recuperating from a back injury.

"I saw all of these books up against the bed, so he can reach them real quick," Wheeler said. "He was reading one of them, and I recognized them as law books. I said, 'What the hell are you doing reading law books?' He said, 'Well, I always wanted to be a lawyer, and I probably should have been, but now all I do is pay them.' And he said, 'If I'm in this hospital long enough, I can educate myself, and I can cut my legal bills in half.'

"I don't even know if he finished high school, but he was as smart as a whip. He was loosey-goosey. He acted like he was never serious about anything, and he *never* was serious around a race car."

Big Bill France kicked Turner out of NASCAR for a while, and Wheeler recalls Turner at Darlington after his comeback. Humpy was then working for Firestone.

"Red Vogt was his crew chief, and Red hadn't gotten to the track yet," Wheeler said. "He was detained for something. So Curtis was heading up things, which was a disaster, because he didn't know anything mechanically about a car. But he was flying around that racetrack. He comes in, and we take a tire temperature."

That's when Wheeler realized that Turner had mounted the left-side tires on the right and the right-side tires on the left.

"That's kinda like replacing a baseball with a basketball," Wheeler deadpanned. "You just can't do that, but he was running faster than anyone on the racetrack. I said, 'Curtis, you got the tires reversed.' He said, 'Well, it's running awful good.' I said, 'But it's not supposed to be like that. You've got the hard tires on the inside and the soft tires on the outside.' He said, 'I guess we ought to fix that, shouldn't we?'

"He got his guys to put them back, and he went out, and he lost a second a lap. And he came back in. He had no idea if he was going fast or not. Ever fast as [the car] would go, that's the way he drove it. I said, 'You lost a half-second a lap,' and he said, 'That's 'cause the tires are screwed up.' I said, 'What do you mean?' He said, 'You put them on the wrong way.' I said, 'No, *you* put them on the wrong way.'"

As Wheeler pointed out, engineers had decided that their way was best.

"But he did it his way, and his way was the fastest," Wheeler said. "He started a storm in the garage area. When you go fast, people find out real quick if it's external because they can see it. If you have some kind of titanium crank in the car, they don't know that.

"So they all wanted to flip their tires, but I knew that if they did that, they'd blister the hell out of them. And we wouldn't let guys do that. Several of them ended up blistering right-fronts.

"But that's just the kind of driver [Turner] was. He didn't pay any attention to what was in the car or on the car. He just drove it as hard as he could."

And he did it even when he was wearing a brown silk suit and wingtips. —T.G.

Bud, Buddy, and Flying Saucers

Paul "Little Bud" Moore was once a Cup driver, but he is not related to the famous Walter "Bud" Moore who owned a race team. This Bud Moore, from Charleston, South Carolina, was and still is a funny guy. In fact, one of his best friends was the always-hilarious Buddy Baker.

Buddy was a test driver for Firestone, and he, Little Bud, and Firestone representative Humpy Wheeler often traveled together.

"Little Bud was one of the funniest drivers we ever had because he was smart as a whip, and he was our first hippie driver," Wheeler said. "We were going to Daytona one night, and we always used to travel to Daytona at night because the South Carolina and Georgia highway patrols didn't operate after 11:00 or 12:00. And the only thing you had to worry about was some deputy sheriff sitting behind a billboard somewhere. We'd be going down on these long back roads. There was a whole network of back roads we used to take."

For some reason the three amigos started talking about flying saucers, which might have been faster than Baker or Moore as they headed to Florida.

"Buddy said, 'Well, I believe in flying saucers,' and Bud said, 'There absolutely can't be flying saucers.' This argument went on for an hour, and I sat and listened to it. They conjectured reasons why there was and wasn't flying saucers. Bud said to Buddy in the back seat, 'If there aren't flying saucers, how come so many people have seen them?' Buddy said, 'That's not the point. There's a difference between seeing [flying saucers] in the sky and one on the ground.' And Bud, in a smart way, said 'How do you know people *haven't* seen them?'"

Buddy said he hadn't seen one; he'd just read all the crazy newspapers in magazine racks.

"Buddy said, 'I'll ask you this,' and that was, 'If there were flying saucers, what do you think they should do?' And Bud said, 'I don't know.' Buddy said they'd talk to us, and Bud asked how they'd talk to us. Buddy said they couldn't [talk to us], and Bud said, 'What do you mean, they can't talk to us?"

And that's when Baker offered his coup de grace.

"Buddy said, 'Have you ever tried to talk to an ant?'" Wheeler said.

That meant that humans would be like ants compared with extraterrestrials.

"And that ended it all," Wheeler said. "I thought that might be the best explanation about flying saucers ever given by anybody in the world." —T.G.

Seeing Is Believing, Sort Of

Ned Jarrett could see everything clearly, and he still didn't believe it.

As he worked through traffic and chased race leader Dick Hutcherson on May 14, 1965, at a .4-mile track at Hampton, Virginia, Jarrett was watching a guy named Billy Wood, someone everybody in the series knew back then.

"He [Wood] felt he had supernatural powers, that he could cause people to wreck or fall out of a race," said Jarrett, a two-time Grand National champion and now retired from a long-time broadcasting career for ESPN. "I never had seen anything to convince me otherwise."

"Wood pulled for me because I bought him lunch or gave him money," Jarrett added seriously. "I wanted him on my side."

Did Jarrett believe in hoodoo?

"I wasn't taking any chances," he said with a nervous laugh.

Each lap as he entered the corner, Jarrett could glimpse the portly Wood waving his arms and gesturing. Billy was getting his point across.

"I knew what he was doing," said Jarrett. "I'd see [car owner Ralph] Moody kidding and laughing, saying, 'You don't have the power!' I learned later that Billy told him that, in the next 10 laps, Hutch would hit the wall in Turn 1. He did, and I won the race."

Wood didn't see everything, though. History says Jarrett took the lead on lap 102 of the 250-lap race, and Hutcherson ran second, a lap down. Elmo Langley was third, a whopping 10 laps down.

Jarrett had a great year, as he won 13 of his 54 starts and copped his second Cup title. —T.G.

Folks, It's Just a Race!

So you think today's race fans are passionate? In 1961 at the Asheville-Weaverville Speedway in North Carolina the fans rioted because they believed they had been short-changed.

The Western North Carolina 500 ended in a standoff between the fans and the racers when the race was halted after 258 laps because of impossible track conditions. The track deteriorated to such a point that it was too dangerous for the race to continue and, during a red-flag period brought on for the clean up of a crash on lap 208, NASCAR executive manager Pat Purcell told the drivers that the race would be halted in 50 laps (which, being over halfway, would make the race official), adding, "I hope you can make it."

During those final 50 laps, the NASCAR officials slipped out of their uniforms and quietly exited the track. When the fans learned that 258 laps was all they were going to get, they revolted.

A truck was dragged across the access road leading to the infield, effectively blocking the exit. One infield denizen approached the mob to act as a mediator, and he was promptly heaved into a lake. Another was tossed over a fence.

Neither the sheriff's deputies nor the North Carolina Highway Patrol was able to restore order, so as twilight approached, Maurice "Pop" Eargle took matters into his own hands.

Eargle, a 6'6", 285-pound crewman on Bud Moore's team, sought reconciliation with one of the leaders of the mob and was poked in the stomach with a two-by-four for his trouble. Eargle grabbed the board and whacked the guy in the head. Shortly after, the crowd broke up and the teams left. Four spectators were treated at local hospitals.

Junior Johnson, incidentally, led all 258 laps, and was awarded the 23rd victory of his career. —J.M. (Fielden, Vol. II, pp. 128)

A Devil of a Ride

David Rogers, the 1994 NASCAR Winston Racing Series champion, didn't know it, but he was in for a devil of a ride.

Rogers was just trying to help some friends qualify an ARCA car at Talladega (Alabama) Superspeedway in the early 1980s.

"It was a reasonably fast car, maybe a top-five car," Rogers recalled. "I had never driven someone else's race car; I was always real hands-on on the setups and all."

In practice, he decided the Buick Regal was running a lot "freer" than it had earlier, so he took the owners' advice and opted for one lap.

He didn't make it. He came off Turn 4 and headed toward the trioval. He prepared to turn; the Regal didn't.

"All of a sudden, everything got real quiet, and I said, 'Oh, gosh, I've seen this on TV before,'" Rogers said with a nervous laugh. "The car lifted up, actually, blew over. I got sideways and all I could see was the sky and grandstands, and I thought, 'Gosh, this is going to hurt.'

"It bounced, and it flounced. The comical part of the whole thing—well, there's two deals. One, I got disoriented. It never knocked me out; the car never hit hard. It was just steady hitting. I didn't realize it, but I'm upside down, sliding across the infield, toward pit road.

"I got my eyes open, and I thought, 'Gosh, I'm going to die.' Everything would get quiet, and then, bam, it'd start hitting again. I'm upside down, sliding across the infield, the windshield's gone. And, all of a sudden, it started getting dark."

Heaven help us! Rogers' vision was going away! No, everything's turning red! Suddenly...it's all black.

"I said, 'You know what? I bet I go to hell.' I kept waiting, at any time, to see this Devil in the darkness. Then, all of a sudden, wham, bam, here I went again. I said, 'Hold on. I'm not dead.' I could see, and the car ended up on the wheels on pit road about 50 yards from where the guy let me go out to qualify. I was headed like I was going back out on the racetrack.

"About 50 yards ahead of me, I could see the coil springs out of the car jumping up and down, and I think, 'Gosh, at least I'm not dead.'"

The ARCA official who had sent him out started toward the car. Suddenly, the official looked horrified, making Rogers wonder if he was disfigured. The stunned man teetered back and sat on the pit wall.

"I started getting my helmet off, and other than being a little shook, I wasn't hurting that bad," Rogers explained. "Another official ran up, 'Stay in the car; you all right?' I said, 'Am I at the racetrack at Talladega?' He said, 'Yeah.' And I said, 'Then I'm all right.'"

While waiting for the ambulance, Rogers walked over to the official on the wall and asked why he was so shaken.

"He said, 'I was walking toward you, and you had the biggest grin on your face,'" Rogers said. "I said, 'Shoot, man, I was just glad to see somebody.'"

Rogers laughed along with the crowd as they pictured a dirty-faced driver sitting in a dented-up race car, with that silly, death-skull smile glued to his mug.

"He thought I was sitting in the car dead with this big grin on my face," Rogers said. It turns out the red Alabama clay had covered Rogers' goggles, at first turning them a reddish—and devilish—hue. Then the goggles went black as they got packed in clay. When his goggles were jostled off, his vision returned.

He recounted finding the evidence, and, again, he laughed in relief.

"It was a good story, because I could tell it, but it was like it was all slow motion," he says. "That was an incredible ride.

"The wreck, after it was over, seemed like it took two days."

As it turned out, the owners of that ARCA car unknowingly made the car unstable. When they were asked what they'd done, they said they blocked off the grill, flattened the spoiler, and increased tire pressure.

"They said they did everything they could do to make the car run faster, when any one of those things would have set the car off," Rogers said. —T.G.

Never Happened—Or Did It?

Sometimes the best stories around NASCAR are the ones you just can't quite nail down as to whether they're really true or not.

A great example of that involves the legend of UPS and its intentions to sponsor a race team years before it got hooked up with Dale Jarrett and Robert Yates Racing.

Supposedly, UPS had entered into negotiations to sponsor a Cup team. The talks had reached a crucial stage—it was time for the parties to exchange paperwork.

So the sponsor sent some material to the team. The team completed the forms and polished up its final proposal. All that was left was for the sponsor to agree to the final terms and the deal was done. So the team's secretary gathered up all of the material for the proposal and shipped it to the good folks at UPS.

Via Federal Express.

End of sponsorship negotiations. —D.P.

The "Real" Kyle Petty

Believe it or not, there was a front-tire changer named Kyle Petty. No fooling.

Here's how it worked out: in 1960 in North Carolina, Richard and Lynda Petty named their son Kyle. In 1972 in Ohio, Steve and Rita Petty named their eldest son Kyle after a TV character.

Years ago, Rita wrote the famous racer a letter, and the Ohio Pettys met the "real" Kyle Petty during a family trip to a Charlotte NASCAR race.

"He came over by the gate where I was standing, and we talked a while," said the "other" Petty. "He was pretty nice and we laughed about our names."

The less-famous Kyle moved to Charlotte in the early 1990s and began working with various race teams. He even worked for Petty Enterprises in 1998.

"We didn't talk too much about it when I worked there," the tire changer said. "I can do his signature, but I sign my last name differently. Sometimes I get Kyle's mail at the house, and NASCAR even sent me a packet of his fan mail that got redirected. I took it to the track and gave it to him."

There is an occasional downside to the name, but Petty tries to take any aggravation in stride.

"It's always been a weird subject," he said. "Sometimes I get tired of hearing that I am the 'other' Kyle Petty. But it doesn't bother me. I like my name." —T.G.

A Car on the Rocks

Maurice "Pop" Eargle was one of the most innovative mechanics on the NASCAR circuit in the 1950s and '60s, and he probably saved the lives of numerous drivers who never even knew him.

Eargle invented an ingenious but simple check-valve (a steel ball from a pinball machine, enclosed in a metal-strap cage) that kept gasoline from leaking out of the tanks of turned-over race cars.

He also invented a "rotisserie" for cars, widely copied, that allowed mechanics to work upright. When working with car owner Cotton Owens, Eargle figured that if he removed the car's bumpers and put the car on a pedestal, then locked it into place, he could rotate the car to any angle the mechanic needed.

Eargle's wizardry included building heavy-duty spindles, racing hubs, fuel and oil tank baffles, spring hangers, and dozens of other innovative pieces.

He was not above a little on-the-spot "engineering," too, when it was necessary. Once, when he was working for car owner Bud Moore, a NASCAR official on pit road measured Moore's car and told him it was too low to pass inspection. While Moore was arguing the point, Eargle, who was standing nearby, found two small flat rocks, stealthily dropped one in front of each front wheel, and rolled the car forward a couple of inches.

Then he told the official that he could have made a mistake and asked him to remeasure.

By then, of course, the car was exactly up to the standard height, and the official walked away scratching his head. —J.M.

Did Somebody Say Cut? Could They?

Most of the time in its history, NASCAR has gotten it right just about every time when it comes to marketing. The sport's incredible growth over its history has been based on a lot of good decisions.

But nobody's perfect.

On May 1, 1998, during the year in which the sport celebrated its 50th birthday, NASCAR gave itself a party in Tinseltown. It was called "NASCAR's Night in Hollywood—A Golden Celebration."

It was, well, it was just bad.

At the Wiltern Theater on Wilshire Boulevard in Hollywood, NASCAR folks rented a lot of fancy clothes and limousines and gathered for what the people putting it on tried very, very hard to make it: a grand affair.

Before the show began, the audience was instructed on how excited they should be. An announcer narrated footage of "Don Allison" and "Dave Pearson" arriving.

You knew it was going to be spectacularly bad when the opening number was—no joke—Robert Goulet and the Anita Mann Dancers performing "That's Why NASCAR is the Champ," to the tune of "The Lady is a Tramp." One snippet? "Big wreck? What the heck! That's why NASCAR is the champ."

Louise Smith, a pioneer female driver in NASCAR's history, was "honored" by Mike Love of the Beach Boys and Dean Torrence of Jan & Dean singing "Little Old Lady from Pasadena," as dancers shimmied in bikini tops while driver Morgan Shepherd joined them on roller skates.

Several awards were presented, including a lifetime achievement award to Richard Petty that was given to him by film director Oliver Stone. You could look a long, long time and not find two men who had less in common, politically or culturally.

"It was something different," Petty said.

Somebody asked him if it was like an out-of-body experience.

"Not out of body," he said, "but definitely out of place."

—D.P.

First, Last, and a Bunch in Between

Ed Clark was in his first year as boss of Atlanta Motor Speedway when one of the greatest races of all time was run. The season-ending race in 1992 was Richard Petty's swan song and Jeff Gordon's first race, and it featured a great championship duel between Bill Elliott and the late Alan Kulwicki.

"Awesome Bill from Dawsonville" in Georgia won both races at Atlanta, his "home track," that year, but Kulwicki didn't make it easy for him. And Kulwicki, who died the next year in a plane crash, "stole" the championship.

About five drivers had a shot at the title with two or three races left, but Kyle Petty and Harry Gant fell out before the season finale. Early in the season ender, points leader Davey Allison got in a wreck, leaving Elliott and Kulwicki to battle it out.

Kulwicki was reportedly having gear problems in that race, making it hard to enter and leave the pits. Elliott led 102 of

328 laps of the Hooter's 500, and Kulwicki led 103 laps. Both men got five points for leading a lap, and Kulwicki got five points for leading the most laps. If Elliott had led one more lap, they would have had to go to a tiebreaker. And with more victories that year, Elliott, not Kulwicki, would have been the 1992 Winston Cup champion.

Petty was involved in a wreck fairly early in the race. He was listed as running at the end, and was credited with 95 laps and a 35th-place finish. Gordon was also in a wreck and finished 31st.

Twenty years and 85 Cup wins (and probably counting) later, Gordon's first race has become a bigger deal; in fact, Atlanta Motor Speedway planned to commemorate Gordon's 20th anniversary in the track's 2012 Labor Day weekend.

Clark remembers that 1992 race for all of the above reasons, and more.

"Three Blackhawk helicopters were supposed to basically hover high above the starting field when they took off, and after a lap they'd leave," Clark said. "Instead, the helicopters stayed right over the rooftops of the cars. They stayed out there for all the pace laps, right until they took the green flag.

"I was in the control tower, through a glass partition right next to [NASCAR boss] Bill France Jr. And when those choppers were that low over the cars and didn't leave, he was trying every way he could to get my attention, because he was not happy about it. I knew he was there, so I was doing everything I could to act like I didn't know he was there and trying to get my attention. I managed that for about three laps, and finally they did leave. They pulled away, and the cars took the green flag, and I kinda looked at him and wiped my brow. Boy, he was red in the face, just steaming."

But that's not the end of the story. Later, Clark got a letter from an irate fan who had been sitting in the bleachers and saw a different beginning to the race.

"He sent me a letter saying that the choppers were so low they had blown his [Dale] Earnhardt cap off, and he had just bought a Coke and hot dog, and he got dirt in his drink and hot dogs," Clark said, "so I sent him a check for something like $32."

Apparently the show, one of the best races ever, wasn't enough. —T.G.

Keep Reaching for the Stars

For more than a quarter of a century, NASCAR races did not start without the approval of Johnny Bruner and, remarkably, all but one of those races finished with his approval.

The Birmingham, Alabama, native's first involvement with racing came in 1937 when he worked as an assistant flagman for midget races at a small New Jersey track, and he found the job to his liking.

"I never got to drive; it just never interested me," he said. "I always wanted to be a starter and nothing else."

His big break came in 1949 when Bill France Sr. asked him if he'd help by flagging the beach races at Daytona. It began a lifelong friendship and a very interesting career.

Back in those days, most flagmen worked the race from trackside instead of in flag stands, and Bruner had his share of moments. He was occasionally bowled over by the midget racers, and he had his feet run over more times than he'd have liked.

But the 1952 beach-road race at Daytona had enough excitement to last him for a while.

"I'll never come any closer to getting the real checkered flag myself than that day," he said. "I had just finished flagging Marshall Teague's winning car when the fourth-place car, driven by Tommy Thompson, lost control. That big Chrysler headed toward me from about 200 yards out, and I started backing away more as a reflex action than anything else."

Bruner almost had it figured out, thinking that the car would drift away out toward the sand dunes, but the tail end caught the pole that held up the start-finish line banner, and it careened wildly in his direction. He didn't have time to run, so he jumped.

"Always jump when something is about to hit you," he said. "Never get caught with your feet on the ground."

Thompson's car hit him and knocked him about 40 feet into the air, but he was uninjured.

"I got up with the flag in my hand and still chewing on my cigar," he said. "I guess Gabriel wasn't quite ready to flag me off for good." —J.M. (Cutter, pp. 95)

Smoked and Fit to Be Tied

Ed Clark, the president for Atlanta Motor Speedway, is always careful when he is in victory circle or the press box after a win. He's especially watchful when Tony Stewart is the Cup race winner at Atlanta, something that's happened three times (spring of 2002, fall of 2006, and fall of 2010).

"Tony Stewart and I have started a tradition; I guess you'd call it a tradition," Clark said. "It's happened twice. After a win, he'll take my tie and take it home and put it in his museum. The first time he did it, it was my favorite tie, so now I don't wear a tie that I like a bunch on Sunday on race day, because I know if Tony wins he's going to end up getting it.

"I didn't want to give it to him the first time; he basically just took it off me. I don't know how amusing [the story] is, but he seems to get great amusement from it."

Maybe Clark ought to start wearing silly ties. Smoke might like Bugs Bunny or Yosemite Sam. —T.G.

"Say What, Bobby?"

There is nothing funny about the crash that robbed veteran driver Neil Bonnett of his livelihood in 1990 at Darlington, nor in the wreck at Pocono Raceway in 1988 that ended Bobby Allison's driving career.

But Bonnett, who later lost his life in a crash while trying to make a comeback in the 1994 Daytona 500, recovered from the near-fatal injury at Darlington, and he once noted that his and Allison's recuperation period did have its moments.

Allison's head injury at Pocono was so severe that he spent months in the hospital and years in recuperation from brain damage. Bonnett suffered temporary amnesia after he wrecked at Darlington and, since he and Allison were both from Hueytown, Allison was the first to check in on his friend and protégé.

The scene, Bonnett recalled later, was poignant, but not without some levity.

"Bobby was the first guy who stopped by my house," Bonnett said. "We were sitting there on the couch. Between Bobby trying to say what he was thinking and me trying to remember what he was saying, it was a helluva conversation." —J.M.

Almost Down the Toilet

This story could have been a real stinker.

Chris Browning is the boss at Darlington Raceway now, but it's still a little embarrassing for him to tell this story about North Carolina Speedway. Browning was in charge at Rockingham in 1996 when they built a new press box and suites. Actually, they built them between the two races, with a tight deadline from the start.

"Everything had to go exactly perfect to get the structure built in the short time frame," Browning said. "We were putting the finishing touches on it during the week of the race. We had practice and qualifying on Friday. Good, no problems. On Saturday, there was the Nationwide race, and we had some plumbing problems in that building. We kept chasing the problem, what's going on, what's going on? We got through the day okay, but we realized there was something pretty major we had to correct before the big race on Sunday, because there were going to be a lot more people in the stands and the suites on Sunday."

They were working overnight on the sewage system to the brand-new $6 million building, and it almost turned into a comedy of errors.

"We worked all night on septic tanks, on this place we had talked so much about and were so proud of," Browning said. "We worked until 2:00 in morning, trying to find the problem. At about 1:00 in morning, still no answers. We got a call saying that the new grandstand in Turn 1 was on fire. We're like, 'Oh, crap.' Me and our superintendent and some maintenance workers jumped into a truck, and we were flying toward the gate to the grandstand. Our superintendent overshoots the gate, hits the brakes, and he slams the thing into reverse, not realizing that one of the other guys was behind him. We drove back into the truck behind us. It tore up the front of that truck and tore up the back of our truck.

"So we limped around to the grandstand, ran up into the grandstand, and realized the grandstand wasn't on fire. The grassy area beside the grandstand was on fire. There were fireworks that somebody shot off, and it had caught the grass on fire. And then we were sitting there thinking, 'You know, we're a bunch of idiots. The grandstand was concrete and steel; it couldn't catch on fire if it had to.'

"That was a long night."

To make a long story short, they had to call a local Porta-John vendor to take care of the toiletry needs that Sunday.

"It was our only option," Browning said. "We did a pretty good job hiding the problem. People think promoting is easy, but trust me there's a lot more to it than you'd think."

Of course they figured out the problem a week later.

"The next week when we had time, we learned that the contractor had drilled through some of the piping when they put in the footings for another part of the building," Browning said. "When they poured the concrete, it filled up a small portion of the plumbing, and obviously the concrete hardened, and [the sewage] didn't have anywhere to go.

"We figured it out, but it was a week too late."

For what it's worth, the show went on pretty well. Forty-two cars started the race, and Ricky Rudd started second and won the AC-Delco 400 in the No. 10 Tide Ford. Ricky and the track came out smelling like a rose. —T.G.

A Barrel of Laughs

The late Benny Parsons grinned sheepishly and squirmed when he told this story from 1972, so it must be true.

Parsons, who would become the Winston Cup champion the very next year, was pitting at Texas World Speedway in College Station. That's the home of the Texas A&M Aggies, of course, and he could have used their help.

It was 105 degrees or so, and the crew handed Benny a water hose that was attached to a 55-gallon barrel. The water, under pressure so it could cool a radiator, served the same purpose for the overheated Parsons. He wet down his suit so that, when he got up to speed, the wind would cool him until his uniform dried.

"Suddenly, the car caught fire, or so I thought," Parsons said, "and they were yelling for me to go, take off!"

Benny threw out the water hose and went busting down pit road—no pit-road speed limit then—and a tiny NASCAR official at the end of the pits dubbed "Short Arms" waved his, well, short arms to put a halt to Parsons' flight. Benny, thinking Short Arms was indicating the fire, charged up onto the banking; the speed, he thought, would kill the flames.

Over the roar of the engine, he heard it.

Boom! Thump! Boom! Thump!

Crash! Bump!

In the banking, he looked back and saw no fire. When he threw the water hose out the window, he realized, it caught on the window net. The net was intact, although mashed down, but that royal-blue, 55-gallon water tank was banging around back there.

Boom! Crash! Boom! Thump!

Fortunately for the abashed Benny, Texas World had fewer than 30,000 fans, and NASCAR had no TV contract then. He drove around the track and back down pit road, then ditched the tank.

Parsons was serious as he talked about that tank swinging back and forth on the water hose.

"That's why people shouldn't stand in the pits," he said. —T.G.

Everything's Bigger in Texas

It might not be in the record books, but the worst traffic jam in the history of motorsports took place in 1997 at Texas Motor Speedway on the morning of the track's first Cup race. People who go to a lot of races gripe about traffic all of the time. But this one was...well...it was just plain biblical.

Imagine traffic on a scale. Zero is an open road. Three is rush hour. Seven is a 20-car pileup. Ten is when a passenger jet makes an emergency landing in rush hour at the intersection of two interstate highways and causes a 20-car pileup. On that scale, the first Texas race was a 50.

To be fair, it wasn't totally the track's fault.

Heavy rain fell for days before the race. On the first day of practice, at one point teams were told to put down all of the lift gates on their haulers and put away all of their equipment because big storms were coming. The radar looked like someone had spilled red paint on it. When the storms arrived that afternoon, they were open for business.

The result of all that rain was that almost all of the parking lots surrounding the track, except for a few thousand paved spaces immediately adjacent to the track, were unusable. The track, which has nearly 170,000 seats, planned for fans to park in fields around the property. But those field were simply too muddy to use.

Everybody knew it was going to be a problem, and the track and local officials tried to line up bus service to shuttle people from usable lots several miles away. But it was the first time any kind of crowd that size would be coming to the track, and even under ideal conditions there would have been some first-time confusion.

This, however, was not ideal.

At 8:00 AM on race morning, traffic was already backing up in virtually every direction and on virtually every road leading to the track, which is located north of Fort Worth. By 10:00 AM, Interstate 35-W, which goes right in front of the track, had turned into a parking lot. People were pulling their cars off to the side of the road, getting out, and walking toward the track. It was faster. The buses that had been arranged to get people to and from the satellite parking lots were stuck in traffic, too.

It's amazing anybody got there that day. It's even more amazing that anybody came back the next year, too, after having to deal with that.

The track itself got its own criticism.

As first designed, Texas Motor Speedway had compound banking. It was relatively flat in the low groove, then banked more steeply in the second and third lanes up. The idea was for Indy-style cars to run on the flatter surface and stock cars to use the higher banking, but the transitions between lanes proved tricky.

There also was a "kink" in the outside wall coming off Turn 4. As cars exited the turn, the wall seemed to almost stick out into the outside groove. From the first time you saw the track, you couldn't help but think how odd it seemed. And drivers complained about it.

So in 1998, when the teams were getting ready to come back for the second year, there was a lot of talk about what might happen. The week before the race, there was talk in the garage area at Bristol Motor Speedway that NASCAR had considered postponing or canceling the race because it had once again been rainy that spring and the track had drainage problems that caused water to seep up through cracks in its surface. One story making the rounds was that when track management drilled a hole to try to assess the problem, a 10-foot high geyser of water sprung out.

"That's the most insane thing I have ever heard," track general manager Eddie Gossage said.

Gossage said there had been some drainage issues that prevented some teams from testing, but ditches had been dug to address the problem. And he was getting a little tired of hearing his track criticized roundly.

"I am not taking a shot at Las Vegas or California or anybody," Gossage said of tracks that were also new at the time. "They are fabulous race tracks and great additions to the circuit.

"But the Blue Angels flying team is exciting because their wing tips are a few feet apart. If they were a half-mile apart, it wouldn't be as interesting."

Early in the week of the 1998 race, Gossage revealed that his track's souvenir department had come up with a new T-shirt. "I expect it to be the first one to sell out this weekend," Gossage said.

On the front, the shirt said, "No Crying." On the back, it said, "Shut up and Drive."

You know where this is going, don't you?

That Friday, there were several crashes in practice for both the Cup and Busch Series, and there were so many crashes in the Busch qualifying that Cup time trails were 90 minutes late getting started. By that time, Turns 1 and 2 were already covered in shade by the grandstands. Early on in the Cup qualifying session, Derrike Cope crashed in that area. Then Lake Speed wrecked.

The next thing you knew, NASCAR officials were standing out in Turn 1 putting their hands and napkins and handkerchiefs down on the racing surface. And they were feeling water seeping up through the asphalt.

Qualifying was postponed until 10:15 AM Saturday.

"What has happened, we believe, is that the race cars form a suction on the race track as they go by and they're pulling [moisture] out as the day goes on," Gossage said. "Once the sun set, it quit evaporating. Plus, we've had 10, 20, 30 cars on it at a time. Now we've got one at a time, so the cars can't dry it as well.

"That's the dilemma we face. It's the first time we've seen this in about a week or 10 days. It's extremely regrettable…but those are the cold, hard facts."

The cold, hard reality, though, was that the drivers were not happy.

"What's frustrating is the drivers posted some concerns about it and hoped they'd listen," Jeff Burton said. "All we get is them printing T-shirts about it saying we need to shut up and drive. That's frustrating."

Ken Schrader was even more blunt. "It isn't going to get fixed without bulldozers," he said. "Not the whole race track, but it needs major work. I don't care what they say."

After that weekend, the track was reshaped. It has been repaved again since, and in the past few years complaints about the track surface have abated.

But those first two years were something to remember.

Going back to that first race in 1997, one of the most unforgettable moments came just minutes before the green flag flew. The track had arranged to have famed concert pianist Van Cliburn perform the national anthem that day. A singer had been booked to do "Yellow Rose of Texas" before that, but after he sang that song he was re-introduced to do the anthem. As he sang, those watching from the press box and suites atop the grandstands could see a flatbed truck driving through the infield with a grand piano on it. The seat was empty.

The singer forgot part of the words to the "Star-Spangled Banner," but in his defense he didn't know until a few minutes before he started singing it he was going to be asked to.

Where was Van Cliburn?

No, he wasn't caught in traffic. Track officials figured that might happen, so they arranged to have a helicopter pick Mr. Cliburn up and bring him in for the pre-race festivities. Well, at least they were supposed to.

Somebody forgot to arrange for the helicopter. —D.P.

A Ghost of a Chance

No, it wasn't Halloween, just a normal race day. One of the weirdest scenes in stock car history came in 1966 when the Northern Tour visited the half-mile Fonda (New York) dirt oval along the Erie Canal.

Richard Petty won the pole, but J.T. Putney led the first 31 laps of the 200-lap, 100-mile race. Then Petty caught up, and the two dueled through the second turn.

Putney's Chevrolet went off the low banking and onto a road paralleling the back straight and the canal. He disappeared for a moment, then reappeared as the leaders entered Turn 3 under the lights. The ensuing crash wiped out five cars and brought out a long caution.

Pace car driver Bob Latford saw the roof number of a car parked nose up on a dirt mound supporting a light pole. He found the track blocked from the inside guardrail to the outer edges, so he turned right, into the darkness.

From the dead end, he ran into a cemetery!

As Latford's car bobbed and weaved through the maze of graves, the stock car drivers obediently followed its taillights. The ghostly procession twice lapped the impromptu off-road course with drivers carefully dodging monuments that might tear up a car and put it out of the race.

Finally, cleanup crews opened a hole in the on-track carnage for the cautious drivers to leave the cemetery circuit.

Years later, I asked David Pearson if he remembered the cemetery. Not a ghost of a chance. Then who won the race, David?

"I don't know," he said. "I guess it was me."

You betcha. —T.G.

Lightning Rods

In 1991, there was an awful thunderstorm at Talladega Superspeedway, with lightning striking in the infield and just outside the track. One of my friends and I were among those stuck in the metal press box, which was too much of a lightning rod for our tastes.

So we rushed out into the monsoon and slid down a muddy bank along with the rushing water. We got into my friend's truck and sat until we could back out. As we drove through the parking lot, we saw a Camaro with water all the way to the top of the tire wells. That thing wouldn't crank anytime soon.

The next day, a Monday, we were in the Talladega infield media center—we weren't going back to the press box, ever—and it was a beautiful day. A crewman, wearing headphones with antennas, was regaling us with stories before the race. He said that during the storm the day before, he was standing near the fuel pumps, and he wondered why everyone was running away from him.

Then he remembered he was wearing mobile lightning rods on his head. Even he had to grin…and shudder. —T.G.

chapter 8
The Family Business

Richard Petty, after winning Daytona 500, 2-14-71

The Pettys. The Allisons. The Waltrips. The Earnhardts. The Bakers.

Stock car racing's history is filled with stories about the sport's famous families.

Honor Thy Father and Mother... Particularly Thy Father

Richard Petty, the "King" of NASCAR racing with 200 victories, is probably the most graceful man to ever wear a racer's fire suit.

In the middle of his remarkable 1967 season, when he won 27 of 58 events and became NASCAR's all-time winningest driver with 55 victories, it was his father Lee Petty's record that he broke.

Appropriately enough, the 55th win came in the Rebel 400 at legendary Darlington Raceway, and perhaps more appropriately, the guy who finished second that day was David Pearson, whose 105 victories would put him in second place behind Petty in career wins.

Despite running into the wall on lap 89 of the 291-lap race, Petty led 266 laps and was more than a lap in front of Pearson at the finish.

When he became NASCAR's all-time winningest driver that hot afternoon in the South Carolina flatlands, his post-race comments were about as graceful as they come.

"There's been a lot of fuss lately over me tying or breaking Daddy's record of 54 victories," Richard Petty said. "We've never even thought of it that way. As far as we're concerned, the Petty family has 109 wins." —J.M. (Fielden, Vol. III, pp. 140)

Check, Please!

Nearly all of the parties involved in the glorious fight after the 1979 Daytona 500 have gotten a ton of mileage out of what many call one of the landmark races in NASCAR history.

Bobby Allison, in fact, says that by his estimation NASCAR has made $53 billion off of what happened after the first Daytona 500 to be shown on live network television.

Donnie Allison and Cale Yarborough wrecked each other on the final lap, allowing Richard Petty to go by and win the race. Bobby Allison pulled his car up to where they'd stopped when the race was over, saying he wanted to see if his brother needed a ride back to the garage. "But then Cale accused me of causing the wreck, and I think I questioned his ancestry," Bobby Allison says. "In fact, I am sure I did."

Bobby Allison said Yarborough came at him and hit him in the face with his helmet, sending blood gushing from Allison's face.

"I had to get out of the car and address it, or run from him the rest of my life," Bobby said. "So I climbed out and my story is he started beating on my fist with his nose."

Yarborough's line is that it wasn't a fair fight—he believed he should have had one hand tied behind his back to fight the two Allisons.

Junior Johnson owned the car Yarborough destroyed in the wreck, and he was a little put out. "I knew what went on out there," Johnson said. "And after it was over, somebody came running up to me in the garage after they wrecked and said they were over there fighting.

"I was asked if I intended to go over there and do something about it. I said, 'Hell, no, let 'em kill each other as far as I'm concerned. The day is over for me.'"

Afterward, NASCAR fined Yarborough and both Allisons $6,000 each for their "actions detrimental to racing," which, given what the incident means to the sport's lore, makes that a fairly laughable phrase.

Prize money in 1979 wasn't what it is today. Two years before that, Allison ran 30 races and earned a total of $94,575 in official winnings. In 2005 Bobby Labonte finished 43rd in the Daytona 500 and won $276,444—almost three times Allison's 1977 annual total.

"We got fined $6,000 apiece," Bobby Allison said. "Donnie and Cale won more than that but I finished 11th and didn't make enough to pay the fine. I had to write a check."

Allison's official winnings that day were $17,725, but after car owner Bud Moore got his share, Allison swears he didn't have $6,000 to pay the fine.

"They refunded the money after we were good boys for the designated amount of time after that," Allison contends. "But they only refunded the prize money they withheld and they never gave me back the check I wrote." —D.P.

Goats, Grass, and Going Fast

It seems that Dale Jarrett almost tried as hard to get out of being a race car driver as his father, Ned, tried to be one. Both of them, however, wound up being NASCAR champions.

Ned Jarrett was the part owner of a race car that ran at Hickory Motor Speedway. His parents didn't mind him owning and working on race cars, but they didn't care for the idea of him being a driver. Race car drivers of that day were known as bootleggers and roughnecks, and those reputations weren't always that far off.

John Lentz, Jarrett's brother-in-law, was driving the car. But one night he got sick, and they decided that Ned should drive the car. Ned did so, without telling anybody, and finished second. Jarrett and Lentz decided that Ned might be a better driver than Lentz, so the next week Jarrett drove again, once again under Lentz's name. He won that week, and when his father found out about it, he told Ned that if he was going to drive he should try to win and certainly should take the credit for it when he did.

So Ned Jarrett officially started his driving career. But it was hardly a lucrative profession, and in 1957 when he wanted to buy a race car for $2,000 that Junior Johnson had driven, he was a little bit short. He was, to be exact, $2,000 short.

He had no money in the bank, but after 5:00 PM on a Friday he gave the car's owner a personal check for $2,000. There were 100-mile races that weekend in Myrtle Beach, South Carolina, and Charlotte, and Jarrett knew that if he won both of them he might come close to covering the check. He did win both races, earning $1,900. He scraped together the remaining $100 and got to the bank bright and early Monday morning.

Ned Jarrett would go on to win 50 races, but he retired as a driver at the age of 33 and went back home to Hickory, North Carolina, where he started promoting races at the track where he'd first raced.

Running Hickory Motor Speedway became the Jarrett family business. But his son Dale was a teenager with other ideas about his life. He'd been a star athlete in high school, playing baseball, football, basketball, and golf. He also had been offered a golf scholarship at the University of South Carolina but decided against going to college. He'd been married and had a son and, at age 20, needed a job. So his father hired him to work at the track.

The younger Jarrett did everything from selling popcorn to driving the pace car at Hickory Motor Speedway, but one of his least favorite jobs was cutting the grass. He decided that what Hickory Motor Speedway needed was some goats to eat the grass he didn't want to cut.

It seemed like a good idea at the time, Dale would say years later. And the goats did eat grass. They also, however, took a liking to the seats and dashboards in some old cars Ned kept on the track's grounds for use in demolition derbies.

"You could say I lacked direction," Dale admits.

At about the same time, he started working on a car that two of his buddies, Jimmy Newsome and future NASCAR crew chief and car owner Andy Petree, had been working on. They wanted to race it at Hickory, but they needed a race engine. Dale asked his father to loan them the money to buy it, and because of that, Dale was elected to be the team's driver.

That first race was a revelation. Dale Jarrett started 25th and finished ninth, and after the race, 1970 NASCAR champion Bobby Isaac came down pit road and found Ned.

"I thought you said Dale was driving that car tonight?" Isaac said.

"He was," Ned said.

"Can't be," Isaac said. "He was too smooth."

Dale Jarrett got out of the car and started looking for his parents. He wanted to tell them that he'd just decided what he wanted to do with his life. —D.P.

Buckshot and the Hulkster

Sportswriters often encountered famous people when we attended races in the 1990s at the Charlotte, Atlanta, and Talladega tracks. I once asked the guy next to me who that famous guy was down at the podium at trackside; he was far from the top row of the press box, and I couldn't see him. He told me it was James Garner, my favorite actor.

Then there was the time we were in the Atlanta Motor Speedway infield media center and the circus showed up. Actually, it was a large, muscular man with a bleached mustache and a canary-yellow outfit, including a head scarf. He swept through the door with dozens of people in his wake.

It was Hulk Hogan, the Hulkster, then the biggest man in wrestling. He was billed as 6'7" and 302 pounds. I doubt he was quite that tall; he looked more like 6'4" or 6'5", but he was tall. He might have weighed more than 302.

It was obvious that some wrestling organization was doing a promotional deal through Petty Enterprises, as Richard Petty and his driver, Roy "Buckshot" Jones, soon showed up.

With cowboy hat and boots, Petty was probably as tall or taller than Hogan, but he looked half as heavy. Buckshot Jones was close to a foot shorter and more than 150 pounds lighter than Hogan.

At first, Hogan did his gruff voice that goes over so well on wrestling programs, but later he sat on a little set of steps and talked in a normal voice about little Terry Bollea growing up in Florida and following wrestling and stock car racing. Maybe it was heartfelt; maybe not, since he was born in Augusta, Georgia. But it was good theater.

Then they decided to take a few publicity shots. Petty and Hogan stood on the top step of the wide little ladder, and Buckshot stood in the front row below them. With Petty smiling the Petty grin, Hogan grabbed Buckshot in what looked like a sleeper hold—Bollea wasn't the only one watching wrestling on TV in the '70s. Buckshot quivered in real or feigned fright—it looked real to me—and the cameras clicked.

Soon, the Hulkster was gone. They told us that another wrestler, Sting, was also in the Atlanta infield, but we never saw him. At least I never did. And I doubt that Buckshot waited around long enough for that, anyway. —T.G.

Like Father, Like Sons

Buddy Parrott remembers the day he fired his son.

"One morning, I heard the most awful squealing sound I have ever heard in my life," Parrott said.

It was 1984, and Parrott was crew chief for Richard Petty at Curb Motorsports.

Soon after the squeal, his secretary hurried into his office. "She had the most beautiful fingernails," Parrott said, "but they were just covered with grease. She was crying, 'Look at my hands!'"

A prankster had squirted grease under the handle on a file cabinet. When the secretary went to pull out the drawer, she came out with fingers full of goop. Parrott called a team meeting, demanding to know who was to blame.

"They were all looking around, and I was looking to see who the heck had done this," Parrott said. "One of them had a little sheepish grin on his face. I knew without even asking, it was Todd Parrott."

That day, Buddy Parrott taught Todd the meaning of a word that Buddy had learned early on during his racing career.

"I've had the opportunity to work with a lot of people," Buddy said. "They came out with this word—'fire,' as in 'getting fired.' That gave me the opportunity to switch around. I got fired, I got rehired."

Buddy rehired Todd a few days after the Great Grease Caper in 1984, and the family has done okay since.

When Jeff Burton got his first career victory in the inaugural Cup race at Texas Motor Speedway in 1997, Buddy Parrott was his crew chief. It was the 45th career victory for Parrott, who has since retired.

Todd worked at Curb and then with Blue Max Racing and Penske Racing South before joining Robert Yates Racing in October of 1995. He served as crew chief for Ernie Irvan for the final two races of that season, then helped Dale Jarrett win a championship in 1999. In 2006, Parrott was crew chief for Bobby Labonte on the No. 43 Dodges owned by Petty Enterprises.

"I grew up in the sport," Todd Parrott said. "When I was growing up, when we were going to Talladega, I would go down a week early and go to Hueytown to spend the week with the Allison boys. I would hang out with Davey and Ronald, Donald and Kenny Allison—Donnie's boys."

Buddy Parrott was a crew chief even before he got the family started in racing.

He grew up in Charlotte and went to races with his buddies, but he also had a job working for Pritchard Paint and Glass Company.

"I was a glass mechanic for nine years," he said. "I had a crew that I worked with, and I got myself up to crew chief there. So, I was a crew chief before I was a crew chief."

Parrott's company opened a new store in Salisbury and he got a chance to move there. In 1968, he met Ross Huggins of Huggins Tire, a company that sold tires to race car drivers.

"Ross and I just hit it right off. He was my kind of guy, the kind who worked hard and played hard," Parrott said. He went to Daytona with Huggins' company that July.

Buddy said he came home and told his wife, Judy, that he was going racing. She thought he meant as a fan. He didn't.

Young Todd was four years old. His brother Brad—who later was a crew chief for the Busch Series team run by Roush Racing for driver Carl Edwards—was still a toddler. All of a sudden, Dad was off driving a tire truck to a different race track each weekend. What followed might diplomatically be called a period of adjustment.

"I came home from Bristol one time, drove the tire truck back," Buddy said. "I opened the door and I said, 'Hello!' The house said, 'Hello!' back, echoing through the rooms. I walked in and there was nothing there. She had moved back to Charlotte and moved everything out. She had just had enough of all of this racing."

Racing did take a toll, Todd Parrott said. "At first, Mom and Dad had a hard time with their relationship because Mom didn't understand why he had to be gone all of the time," Todd said. "When I was growing up, he was gone a whole lot. We didn't get to go to baseball games and stuff like that and spend time together with me growing up. I don't have any resentment about it, but I didn't get to know my dad like a lot of people do."

Buddy and Judy Parrott were separated for about a year, then put things back together. Judy came to understand the sport that had a hold on her husband and was pulling her sons toward it. She eventually helped form a public-relations company that handled race teams, and racing truly became the family business.

Todd chose racing over a possible career as a golf pro. "After graduation, I thought, 'Man, what am I going to do now?'" he said. "I had two or three small colleges call and offer me scholarships to play golf. But I was the kind of person who liked playing golf and I didn't like the books."

Todd continued his education, however, learning how to make cars go fast.

"I had the best teachers in racing to learn from," he said. "Barry Dodson, Jimmy Makar, Rusty Wallace, Robin Pemberton, I can't say enough for what they did for me."

While Todd was learning the ropes, Buddy was finding success as crew chief for Bob Whitcomb's team with Derrike Cope as the driver. They won the Daytona 500 in 1990.

Their careers crossed paths again when both worked at Penske South. Buddy came on as crew chief in 1992 and was there for the following two seasons. That team won 19 races. Wallace finished second in the 1993 points race, losing to Dale Earnhardt by 80 points.

"One night late, I was putting a carburetor together and he [Todd] broke something off on it, something I had asked him not to do," Buddy recalled. "I think it was a 4' level that I threw at him. Everybody still says it sounded like a helicopter taking off as it went over the top of his head going whoomp, whoomp, whoomp."

Parrott's first full season as a crew chief could not have started better. Jarrett won the 1996 Busch Clash and came back a week later to win the Daytona 500. —D.P.

Davey Allison Goes to School

Bobby Allison looked at the young fellow sitting beside him during the post-race interview following the 1988 Daytona 500 and grinned. Then he asked the question that was on everyone's mind: "What I want to know is, would you have passed your dad if he'd let you?" the elder Allison said.

Davey didn't blink. "Without a doubt," he said. "Without a doubt."

One of the most compelling things about auto racing is that it is one of the few sports in which brothers compete against brothers on a regular basis, and occasionally, fathers against sons. But seen through the prism of time, the battle between Bobby and Davey Allison that February afternoon was a classic in every sense.

Bobby Allison was only a few months away from having a crash at Pocono, Pennsylvania, that would end his racing career, and young Davey's star was just beginning to rise. Accidents that would take the lives of both Davey and his brother Clifford were years away, and the future never looked rosier for the Allison clan.

There had been other father-son match-ups. Buck Baker regularly roughed his boy Buddy up whenever the two were on the same track, and Lee Petty never gave Richard a break when the two were fighting for a position. Richard, in his turn, never cut Kyle Petty any slack.

There had been two father-son 1–2 finishes (with Lee Petty beating Richard twice) prior to the Allisons' duel at Daytona. But in most of those instances, the fathers held the upper hand, both in equipment and racing savvy, and the battles were more skirmishes than fight-to-the-last-ditch struggles.

Behind the wheel, the Allisons were as close to equals as you could get.

The Daytona 500 was, and is, the biggest stage in stock car racing. The winner's name is automatically included in any list of racing's great drivers. Bobby's name was already on that list, twice, and that week in 1988 he had won every race in which he was entered at Daytona.

The sense of drama on Sunday was heightened when Davey Allison crashed his car in the final practice on Saturday afternoon, and his crew worked most of the night to get it back into shape.

It was a great race and a great finish. Bobby stood off a last-ditch attempt to pass by his son and beat him by 2½ car lengths at the checkered flag. No chicanery, no blocking out. Just outrunning.

"My whole career, I've done my best to play it straight," Bobby said. "And when you are racing against the best youngster to ever come along, you wouldn't want to do anything other than that."

Still, Davey wondered aloud what might have happened if his car hadn't been damaged on Saturday. Bobby, eyeing the 30-race campaign ahead, looked at his son and grinned.

"You've got 29 more times this year to find out," he said.

—J.M.

chapter 9
Life in Technicolor

*H.A. "Humpy" Wheeler
(right) with Elliott Sadler*

Former Charlotte Motor Speedway president H. A. "Humpy" Wheeler likes to tell people that a race promoter's job is to provide a little "Technicolor" for people who lead black-and-white lives.

If stock car racing had a P. T. Barnum, it was Wheeler. Once, in fact, he heard a couple of sportswriters griping about one of his lavish pre-race extravaganzas. "They might as well have a circus," one said. The next year, the pre-race show was, literally, a circus.

Humpy, DW, Cale, and the Shark

Humpy Wheeler always did things big when he was Charlotte Motor Speedway's president from 1975 to 2008. When he held the Memorial Day weekend extravaganzas for the Coca-Cola 600, they'd blow stuff up and have jets doing fly-bys. One year, they built a house across the way on a hill just so they could blow it up as part of "field exercises." Another year, they had two Huey helicopters fly into the infield, and one turned its guns—we assume they weren't loaded—toward the press box and control tower. Tense moment.

They'd have cars or motorcycles jump something. Adam Petty, long before his death, once drove a big-wheeled vehicle over a bunch of cars. Wheeler, once a Golden Gloves boxer in South Carolina, brought exhibition matches to the speedway.

They'd bring the car-eating metal monster, Robosaurus, into the infield to entertain the crowd. One time, Robo did his work and stopped, and Dale Earnhardt got out.

Wheeler says he always liked to inject humor into racing, and most of his stunts were pretty funny. One year, Rusty Wallace drew a fine—probably $5,000—from NASCAR, and Wheeler had a Brinks truck bring bags of pennies to the track. That got tongues a-wagging, and pictures hit the newspapers.

One of Wheeler's best stunts came at the expense of Darrell Waltrip and Cale Yarborough. DW was a big talker back in the 1970s, so much so that Yarborough nicknamed him "Jaws" after the monstrous shark movie.

So Wheeler, the young president and promoter for CMS, decided to get clever. Or so he thought.

"I called a friend of mine on the [North Carolina] coast, and he'd caught a big, black-tip shark, about a 150-pounder," Wheeler once said. "We put it on the bed of a truck on ice and got it here. On qualifying day, we got some chicken stuffed in its mouth.

"The wrecker driver would take the shark into the pits where everybody was posting times. It was a dead shark, but it was fresh. Both of them [Cale and Darrell] were as mad as the dickens. It was good, though, because it got everybody talking."

Wheeler was inducted into the International Motorsports Hall of Fame on April 27, 2006, and the Motorsports Hall of Fame of America on August 12, 2009.

The shark didn't make it. —T.G.

One Must Die

Humpy Wheeler remembers going to sports events when he was a kid and being bored as he waited on the game or the race to begin. He never could figure out why there was nothing going on.

He's always tried to remember that, he says, in his career as a track promoter. There's almost always something going on somewhere at Wheeler's track.

Most of his ideas are good ones. Some of them, however, don't work out. There was, for example, the time he tried to break the world record for assembling the world's largest marching band. He invited high schools to send their bands to his track before a race, and dozens of them did. There were hundreds and hundreds of teenagers all over the place, all decked out in their full uniforms—many of which were woolen.

As it turned out, the day of the race came up sunny and very, very warm. And as the bands stood on the track waiting for their part of the program, it got pretty hot in those wool uniforms. Too hot, in fact, for some of the students.

"They were dropping like flies," Wheeler said.

Wheeler also liked having a swimmer from the little town he grew up in, Belmont, North Carolina, come over to the track during race weeks and try to break world records. The swimmer, whose nickname was "Moon," was actually a specialist in treading water. For hour after hour, Moon would tread water. And he'd do it longer than anybody ever had.

It was quite an accomplishment, no doubt, but it frankly was not terribly thrilling. Wheeler was looking for a little something to spice up Moon's act, and he was talking to his staff about it one day in a meeting.

"I know," one of his assistants said, "let's put a shark in there with him. You know—Moon versus the Shark: One Must Die!"

The movie *Jaws* was out and everyone got a big laugh out of the suggestion. But Wheeler wasn't laughing. The idea, he thought, had merit. His staff was mortified. "We can't do that!" they insisted.

Wheeler wasn't crazy. But he was thinking outside the box. "We could put him in a chain mail suit, couldn't we?" he said.

Eventually, the staff won out. And Moon never had to face the shark. —D.P.

Isaac's Watch

Bobby Isaac is well known for parking his race car during a race at Talladega Superspeedway in 1973 and later saying that a voice told him to do it. But there's a little more to the story than that.

Humpy Wheeler's favorite Bobby Isaac story is one about a watch Isaac got, ironically, from officials at the Talladega track. After the Talladega incident when a voice told him to park his race car, Isaac quit racing for a while, and he later wound up racing at short tracks like Hickory Motor Speedway near his home in North Carolina.

"One of the results of Talladega," Wheeler said, "was that he didn't want anything in the house that said Talladega. Bill France [Sr.] gave him a gold Rolex watch, and on the back it said 'Quitters never win, winners never quit, Talladega 500.'

"Bobby never wore that watch, never put it on. One day he came into my office [at Charlotte Motor Speedway]. He never knocked on the door. He said he had the watch and said, 'You want you to buy this watch, you need a Rolex?' I said, 'No, I don't.' He said, 'I know you do.'"

Isaac left the watch in Wheeler's drawer and walked out. Later, "Tiger" Tom Pistone called and told Humpy that he owed a certain amount for car parts. Isaac had said that Wheeler would pay for the parts, and Humpy knew that was the cost of the watch.

"I started wearing it, and when he died, I offered to give the watch back to his wife," Wheeler said. "I thought it ought to be part of his trophy collection, but she said, 'No, he wanted you to have it.' It meant more than the money, so I still had it."

Why is Hickory Motor Speedway important? Isaac died after an August 14, 1977, race at Hickory. He was buried August 16, 1977, the day that Elvis Presley died, on a hill behind the Hickory track. —T.G.

Head Games

Buddy Baker had started driving for car owner Ray Fox and he was looking for that little bit extra that he hoped would help him become a winning NASCAR driver. Humpy Wheeler convinced Baker that some extra physical conditioning would do the trick. Wheeler, who'd been an amateur boxer, convinced Baker that they should do some sparring. Wheeler told Baker that if they worked out every day for two weeks leading up to an October race in Charlotte, he guaranteed that Baker would win the race.

The weather still can be rather warm in the Carolinas in October, and it was that year. Still, Baker and Wheeler would turn the heat up in their car as they rode to a field where they would run a little and then spar a little. Baker says his pants were getting too big for him and his stomach was getting harder and harder.

On the day before practice for the Charlotte race began, Wheeler and Baker had one last workout planned.

"Just as we were going to start working out, he said, 'No hitting in the head;'" Baker said. For two weeks, nobody had hit anybody in the head, so Baker thought that was odd. It seemed even more odd when the first time Wheeler took a swing, he hit Baker in the right ear.

"When he did, I was like, 'Okay, let's go,'" Baker said.

Baker and Wheeler went at it, chasing each other through the field and across the road into a man's yard.

"About that time, Humpy put his gloves up and said, 'We'd better stop before somebody gets mad,'" Baker said.

"I said, 'To hell with you, I've been mad since we left that field over there!'"

That was the end of the fight.

But Baker won the race that week. —D.P.

Jimmie Johnson, Hands of Stone

Humpy Wheeler, the erstwhile promoter at Charlotte Motor Speedway and a huge boxing buff, says that Jimmie Johnson can take a punch. And hand one out.

"Jimmie moved to the Charlotte area, and he was working out at Walt Smith's gym. Walt's now the head pit-crew guy for Hendrick [Motorsports], and most of the drivers around Lake Norman worked out at Walter's, because [teams] didn't have gyms at the shops like they do now. And Jimmie was one of them."

Humpy, who also sparred with Hall of Fame driver Buddy Baker and others, says he made the mistake of talking Johnson into going a few rounds.

"I said to him, 'I don't know how tough you are, and you have to be awful tough to run NASCAR,'" Wheeler said. "'Guys will put you in the wall, and you'll have to have something back for them.' Jimmie never brags, but he said, 'I think I can hold my own.'

"So I said, 'Why don't you let me teach you how to box,' and he said 'Okay.' So that was kind of a mistake, because it didn't take long to teach him. It got to where I wasn't looking forward to sparring with him a whole lot, because he could hit.

"Boxers are people who can either hit hard right away or they never will be able to; you'll know right away if a person's got any aptitude [for boxing] or not. He gave me a fit quite a few times. I look back now, and I see people talking about how meek and mild he seems to be, but I'll tell you flat out, he isn't.

"And one day one of these guys will find out when they put him into the wall real hard."

So if you're thinking of getting into an altercation with Johnson in Turn 3 (as in the 1979 Daytona 500), stay in your car and keep going. There's nothing to see here. —T.G.

Let There Be Lights

On their own, Humpy Wheeler and T. Wayne Robertson each had their brilliant moments. Put them in a room together, however, and something memorable was almost bound to happen.

Such was the case at a 1991 meeting in Robertson's office in Winston-Salem, North Carolina. But that's getting ahead of the story.

Wheeler was president of Charlotte Motor Speedway and, since shortly after he was out of college at the University of South Carolina, he was in the stock car racing business in one form or another.

Early on, for instance, Wheeler was running Robinwood Speedway, a dirt track in Gastonia, North Carolina. One weekend his water truck broke down and Wheeler was in desperate need of a tanker he could use to prepare the racing surface. He called a buddy who worked for a septic tank company and borrowed that truck, but at the race that night, his patrons couldn't help but notice the foul residual odor the truck had left behind. Wheeler took to the track's public address system and blamed the smell on an unprecedented wind shift that was carrying the odor in from a nearby pulp mill, which, of course, was not really nearby at all.

Robertson, meanwhile, started out in the marketing arm of R.J. Reynolds Tobacco Company as a driver of one of the "show" cars that went around to supermarket openings and things of that nature to promote the company's sponsorship of NASCAR's top series.

With boundless enthusiasm and a knack for tackling every challenge as though it were a great opportunity, Robertson moved up through the ranks and wound up as president of Sports Marketing Enterprises. No idea was too big, no plan too grandiose for Robertson if he thought it would help NASCAR and the Winston Cup Series grow and gain acceptance.

One story about Robertson sums up his approach to life. One day he was trying to get into Atlanta Motor Speedway to take part in the pre-race ceremonies, but he was stuck in traffic. Robertson "urged" his driver to circumvent the normal pattern set up for ingress to the track, so they were heading down the median when a local traffic enforcement officer took notice...and umbrage.

The officer pulled over Robertson's car and headed over to speak to the driver. But he never got a chance. Virtually before the car was stopped, Robertson bounded out.

"Where have you been!?" Robertson asked. "We've been looking for you for miles!"

The officer was flummoxed, having no idea what Robertson was talking about.

"You're our escort, right? We've got to get inside that track so they can get this race started on time," Robertson said.

The officer bought the bluff and Robertson not only had permission to bypass the traffic he'd been fighting, but he also had help doing it.

In 1985 Robertson and his RJR staff came up with the idea of a big-money all-star event for NASCAR's top series. The inaugural event was set for May at Wheeler's track in Charlotte, and the hype was right down Wheeler's alley. It was a big success, too, with Darrell Waltrip winning the inaugural event.

The idea was to move the race around to different tracks, the way other sports put their all-star games in various places. The second year, it was scheduled for Mother's Day at Atlanta Motor Speedway. That's the day everyone in NASCAR discovered that it wasn't a good idea to race on Mother's Day. The joke was that it would have taken less time to introduce the fans to the drivers than it would have to introduce the drivers to the fans.

So the all-star event returned to Charlotte in 1987 and staged one of the most memorable events in NASCAR history—known for Dale Earnhardt's "Pass in the Grass" where he maintained the lead (it never was actually a pass) despite being run across the corner of the infield grass in the track's trioval.

That was the first year of a five-year contract between RJR and the Charlotte track, a deal that ended with the 1991 running of The Winston.

And that brings us to the aforementioned meeting in Robertson's office in 1991.

It was time to negotiate a new contract. Robertson, frankly, wasn't sure the all-star race needed to continue anywhere. He was afraid it had lost its sizzle but was willing to listen to Wheeler's ideas. Wheeler had a lot of ideas. But he could tell that none of them were doing anything to capture Robertson's imagination.

"I kept throwing things at him, and nothing was getting to him," Wheeler said.

Until, that is, the light went on.

Actually, until the lights went on.

Wheeler told Robertson that he wanted to hold the all-star event on a Saturday night, under the lights. It was a return to racing's roots since short tracks had long run under the Saturday night lights. Robertson loved the idea.

What made Wheeler's idea so revolutionary was the fact that no track as large as the 1.5-mile Charlotte track had lights.

Until the moment the words came out of Wheeler's mouth, his staff had no idea Wheeler had planned to propose lights for the track. There was a good reason for that—Wheeler thought of it on the spot.

"I told them I didn't have the slightest idea how we were going to do it, but we were going to do it," Wheeler said.

The trouble was that lighting a track the size of Charlotte was a considerably more difficult matter than simply putting up light posts. Cars enter the track's turns at better than 180 mph, and at that speed any pockets of dark and light appear as strobe lights—and that wouldn't work. Glare and shadows were also potential issues.

Wheeler had some ideas, including a wide band of light placed atop the wheel fence. He set up a test in Turn 1 and then realized he had a problem.

"I brought a bunch of people in," Wheeler said. "We were going to test in the pace car, and everybody was looking at me like, 'Who's going to do this?' I had to do it, and I almost killed myself. I went down into the first turn and, I'm telling you, I couldn't see anything."

Eventually it took Musco Lighting, a company from Iowa that specialized in stadium-lighting projects, to provide a solution. The company built a one-fourth scale model of Turn 4 at the Charlotte track in an airport hangar near its headquarters to test the system it invented, which features lights bounced off mirrors. Musco wound up getting more than a dozen patents for things it invented to complete the system.

"As soon as I saw it, I said, 'How simple!'" Wheeler said. "I knew it would work." —D.P.

Smoking the Competition

The late Ralph Seagraves may have been the man most responsible for R.J. Reynolds' sponsorship of the Winston Cup Series, the Winston Racing Series, drag racing, and golf. Plus, he created the Winston Cup points fund.

"Basically, everyone liked Ralph," said Bob Moore, who joined RJR's Special Events division right after it was formed in the early 1970s. "He was always selling the sport and RJR; he was always on. It didn't make a difference, day or night or evening, social function, racetrack or business meeting. He was always selling."

"He had a great impact on the whole business," said Humpy Wheeler, the president of Charlotte Motor Speedway from 1975 to 2008. "Ralph was the first person in a major company outside of consumer automobiles or tires to be into sports marketing. He wrote the book on consumer sports marketing, at least the first chapter, anyway."

Seagraves was gregarious and always pushing the Winston brand.

Seagraves, for instance, was leaving promotional cigarettes in the Oval Office at the White House when President Kennedy was assassinated in 1963. The reason? Jackie Kennedy smoked Salems. In fact, Seagraves was detained for several hours when the White House was cordoned off following Kennedy's death.

There's another Seagraves/White House story...

When President Carter invited NASCAR to the White House in the 1970s, the president couldn't make it, but the First Lady stood in for him. Rosalyn Carter was a trouper as Seagraves introduced her to virtually everyone in stock car racing. —T.G.

chapter 10

Gone Too Soon

*Alan Kulwicki, after winning Winston
Cup Championship, 11-15-92*

There's a gap in NASCAR's history that will never be filled. One thing many of the sport's greatest stars have shared in their careers is longevity. A racer can compete from his early twenties on into his mid- to late-forties —and even longer for a select few.

But then there are those whose careers are cut short by tragedy.

Tim Richmond, who died of AIDS in 1989, was on the brink of becoming a breakout star with Hendrick Motorsports.

Alan Kulwicki had won the 1992 Cup championship in improbable fashion, driving for a team he owned himself, but in early 1993 he died in a plane crash. And Davey Allison, the son of champion driver Bobby Allison, had already become one of the sport's most popular young stars when he was killed in the crash of a helicopter he was piloting, also in 1993.

Their deaths were tragic, as were the deaths of great drivers like Joe Weatherly, Fireball Roberts, and Dale Earnhardt. Those three, though, were around long enough that fans got to see just how great they really were. With Richmond, Kulwicki, and Allison, however, the story is how so much seemed to still be ahead of them.

Here, we offer a story about each of these drivers that speaks more about how they lived than how they died. The sport will always miss them.

More Than One Way to Skin a Cat

Rick Hendrick's career as a Winston Cup team owner got off to an interesting start.

Hendrick had owned speedboat racing teams, but got out of that sport when a driver of one of his boats was killed in an accident. Hendrick was looking for a place to store his boats when he learned about Harry Hyde, a former crew chief who'd had great success with former champion Bobby Isaac but had fallen out of favor in the NASCAR garage.

Hyde was looking for one more chance to succeed at the sport's top level, and he saw Hendrick as a ticket to get it. Hendrick was on his way to becoming one of America's top automobile dealers, and he'd grown up interested in racing. Despite the lingering pain from the tragedy with his boat team, he wasn't a hard sell for Hyde.

In 1983 Hendrick had decided to give NASCAR a try. He was working on a deal that would have given him Richard Petty as his driver and country music star Kenny Rogers as a co-owner.

"We were going to have the king of stock car racing [Petty] and the king of country music," Hendrick said of the team, which was called All-Star Racing.

But, as sometimes happens with big deals, things fell apart when it came down to the details. Hendrick wound up going to the 1984 Daytona 500 with Geoff Bodine, whose background was in the NASCAR modified series in the Northeast, as his driver and no sponsor to help him pay the bills. But Bodine won at Martinsville early in that first season, and All-Star Racing found its footing. By the end of the team's second season, the newly named Hendrick Motorsports had picked up a second sponsor, and Hendrick hired Tim Richmond to drive that car.

He'd also hired Gary Nelson to be a crew chief, but decided that Nelson and Bodine would be a better fit. That left Hyde to run the new team with Richmond. Putting together a grizzled veteran crew chief with a flashy, cocky young driver whose reputation as a party-loving, skirt-chaser gave Hendrick's sponsors some concern.

One of the first appearances Richmond was scheduled to make for the sponsor, Folgers Coffee, was in New Orleans. Richmond arrived the night before and met up with a couple of girls in an airport bar. He took them to his hotel, but they slipped him a "mickey" and took his money and watch.

The next morning, at the appearance, everybody was there except Richmond. Someone was dispatched to the hotel, and Richmond was roused from his artificially deepened sleep. He dressed and hurried to the Folgers appearance but quickly minimized the damage with some self-deprecating humor. "If Folgers can get me up to get here this early, you know it's good," he said.

As many people expected, however, Richmond and Hyde didn't get along well from the start. Hyde believed Richmond didn't know how to drive within the limits of control, while Richmond thought Hyde couldn't build him a car good enough to match his driving talents.

Three things happened to turn things around.

First, Hendrick played some head games with his veteran crew chief. Nelson and Bodine both had innovative minds, and both had started putting some things on their team's cars that Hendrick thought might work for Hyde and Richmond, too.

One night, Hendrick had Nelson go home early, and he brought Hyde over to Bodine's shop. He showed Hyde some of the things Nelson was doing to the cars, but Hyde ridiculed or dismissed it all. It would never work, Hyde huffed.

But, Hendrick said, over the next few races at least some of the stuff Hyde had seen that night wound up showing up in Richmond's cars.

The second thing that helped clear the air was an argument that took place in the trailer Hyde used as his office. Richmond and Hyde started at each other, and Richmond finally told Hyde that if he stepped outside the trailer, he'd whip Hyde's tail. Hyde got up and headed for the door, ready to go.

Richmond, however, started laughing. That just made Hyde angrier. But Richmond was beyond fighting. He'd figured out that no matter what happened, he couldn't win a fight with a man more than twice his age. If he'd won the fight, he was picking on an old man. If he lost the fight, he'd had his tail whipped by an old man. Either way, not good.

That incident, though, seemed to break the ice. Not long after that, the team went to North Wilkesboro Speedway in North Carolina, and Hyde figured out a way to show Richmond something he'd been trying to tell him. He had Richmond make a 50-lap run the way Richmond was used to driving the car. Then, he asked Richmond to run 50 laps the way Hyde wanted him to run—backing off a little earlier going into the turns and trying to take care of the tires.

After 50 laps each way, the tires from Richmond's run were a smoking mess. The tires off the run from Hyde's approach still had some good laps in them. And, on the stopwatch, Hyde's way had been quicker.

Richmond finally got it. From that point on, he and Hyde became the story of the 1986 season. Richmond won six races that summer. —D.P.

Radar Love

Over the past 10 to 15 years, more and more NASCAR drivers, owners, and crew chiefs have acquired motor homes that allow them to stay right at the race track instead of fighting the traffic coming in and leaving the track each day.

It's become quite the "arms race," frankly, with each person seemingly trying to find the bus with the most high-tech gizmos and the most expensive toys. Satellite dishes, allowing the NASCAR glitterati access to hundreds of channels for their plasma-screen televisions, are a must. Speed Channel, undoubtedly, has pretty good ratings in the motor home park. Racers love to watch other racers compete.

But another channel that's big in the motor-homes is The Weather Channel. Weather is important to racing, not only because rain means no practice or no qualifying or no race, but because engines and cars behave differently in cold weather than in heat or when it's cloudy or sunny. Several drivers are pilots, too, and pilots need to have a certain fascination with weather to help keep them flying.

It's easy to forget, though, that everybody in racing wasn't always a meteorologist. Just ask Larry McReynolds.

McReynolds, who has been an analyst for FOX Sports' NASCAR broadcasts since 2001, enjoyed a long, successful career as a crew chief. In 1992 he was working at Robert

Yates Racing as crew chief on the No. 28 Fords driven by
Davey Allison.

The '92 season had been remarkable, in good ways and
bad ones, for McReynolds and Allison. They'd won the
Daytona 500, for starters, but in April Davey's grandfather,
Edmund Jacob "Pop" Allison, died.

Allison then won the Winston 500 at Talladega, giving him
victories in the first two of the four races that made up the
"Winston Million," a bonus plan from R.J. Reynolds Tobacco
that paid a $1 million bonus to any driver who could win three
of those races—the Daytona 500, the Winston 500, the Coca-
Cola 600 at Charlotte, and the Southern 500 at Darlington.

Before Allison could worry about trying to win the $1
million at Charlotte in May, he competed in the first all-star race
held under the track's new lights. It was promoted as "One
Hot Night," and it lived up to that billing.

Allison had won the all-star race the previous year and
started on the pole in 1992. By late in the final segment, which
is where the $200,000 first prize was paid, he was third
behind Kyle Petty and Dale Earnhardt.

On the final lap, Petty and Earnhardt made contact in Turn
3 as they fought for the lead. Earnhardt spun and was out of
contention, but because Petty had to slow so dramatically to
keep from wrecking, too, Allison caught up, and Petty began
trying to block him off the final turn. They were side-by-side
coming to the finish line, with Allison a nose ahead just as they
took the checkered flag. Their cars made contact, and Allison
piled into the wall, driver's side first.

Allison had been knocked out momentarily, but he came to
about the time McReynolds got to his car.

"I knew he wasn't hurt-hurt," McReynolds said. "But I knew he was knocked kind of coo-coo."

McReynolds watched the emergency workers cut Allison from the car, but he also kept one eye on the scoreboard. He wanted to see what car number wound up at the top when NASCAR officials finished reviewing the finish.

"It seemed like it took about two hours, and it was probably two minutes," McReynolds said. "Finally, they flipped that No. 28 up top. It was like, 'Yes!'"

Allison had a concussion and several other injuries. Instead of going to victory lane, he got a ride in an ambulance to the infield care center and, later, to a local hospital.

"What happened?" Allison said to McReynolds as they rode toward the infield care center.

"You won the race, Davey," McReynolds said.

"You're shittin' me," Allison said.

"No, Davey, you won the race," McReynolds repeated.

"You're not shittin' me?" Allison asked again.

"Davey, I wouldn't shit you about something like that," McReynolds said. "You won the race."

Earnhardt came back the next week to win the 600, though, denying Allison his first shot at the Winston Million.

Later that summer, Allison was one of the drivers taking part in a "tire test" at Indianapolis Motor Speedway, the first time stock cars had ever been there and a precursor to the Brickyard 400 that would begin in 1994.

In July at Pocono, Allison's car was strong, but a mistake on a pit stop had him back in traffic. As he tried to come back to the front, though, on lap 150 he went into Turn 2—the same turn where his father, Bobby, had suffered career-ending

injuries in a crash four years earlier—and got hit by Darrell
Waltrip.

Allison's car turned sideways and went into the grass, then
flipped backward and began a violent series of 11 barrel rolls.
Amazingly, Allison survived. He was beaten and bruised and
spent the next week in the hospital. He flew back to Alabama
on Friday, determined to be in his car for the start of the next
race at Talladega so he'd get the points and stay in the
championship battle.

Allison had suffered a broken right wrist in the crash at
Pocono. "We had to put Velcro on the palm of his racing glove
pulled over his cast and on the shifter," McReynolds said. "The
only way he could shift was to have his hand Velcroed to the
shifter." That helped him get to the first yellow flag in the race
on Sunday.

The next month at Michigan, Allison's brother, Clifford,
wrecked during a Busch Series practice session and was
killed.

So by the time Allison, McReynolds, and their team got to
Darlington for the Southern 500 on Labor Day weekend, they'd
already been through a lot. Now, they had a chance to become
the first team since Bill Elliott's in 1985 to win the $1 million
bonus.

When Elliott had won the $1 million in 1985, the number
on the roof of his car had been accidentally affixed upside
down. McReynolds had the No. 28 affixed to Allison's Ford
that same way this time, trying to think of everything possible
to help his driver.

Allison had been in contention all day, and as the final 100
miles of the Southern 500 approached, McReynolds faced a

crucial decision. The No. 28 Ford needed fuel, but bad weather was threatening, and if rain was going to cut the race short, Allison needed to stay out as long as he could.

McReynolds motioned one of his team's members over to him and hollered toward him over the pit road din.

"Go check the radar," he ordered.

The team member ran off toward the NASCAR truck, which had a weather radar monitor. A few more laps, and a few more gulps of fuel, passed before his return.

"It looks good," the team member said.

Thus advised, McReynolds ordered Allison to come to pit road for enough fuel to go the full 500-mile distance.

A few laps later, the rain started.

It didn't last long, but it had rained enough and it was getting late enough in the day that NASCAR chose not to restart the race. Waltrip, who hadn't pitted, was declared the winner.

McReynolds, of course, was confused. He found his weather messenger and asked for an explanation. The crew member could not understand what went wrong. He'd gone to the truck and looked at the radar.

"There was green everywhere around us," he told McReynolds.

In racing, of course, green means go. On that radar, though, it had meant rain. If only McReynolds' messenger had known that. —D.P.

Ol' Blue Eyes

Alan Kulwicki went into the final race of the 1992 just 30 points behind Davey Allison in the race for the Winston Cup title.

Bill Elliott was just 10 points behind Kulwicki, and there were also three other drivers mathematically eligible to win the championship after the Hooters 500 at Atlanta Motor Speedway.

NASCAR had never seen anything like this championship battle. And it wasn't like there wasn't anything else to talk about going into that race, either. It was going to be the last race that Richard Petty, the sport's all-time winningest driver, competed in. The sport had spent the entire season saying good-bye to its "King," but the final weekend was going to be special. Petty was going to be the focus of all sorts of activities and ceremonies, including a big party televised on national cable TV on the night before the race.

With the championship race so close, however, there was almost too much going on for everyone to digest. It wouldn't be until several years later that the significance of the fact that the Hooters 500 was also Jeff Gordon's first career Cup race could be fully appreciated.

Elliott had been well ahead in the standings with just six races left in the season, and Kulwicki dropped so far behind even he felt like his chances to win a title had slipped away. After a wreck at Dover, he was 278 points behind and all but convinced it was over.

But Kulwicki hadn't made it to where he was by giving up. He'd run almost an entire season with just one race car after moving to North Carolina from Wisconsin to go racing. He'd also turned away from a chance to join car owner Junior Johnson's super team, in large part because he just didn't think he could do things the way he wanted to do them if he was driving another man's cars.

As the principal players began to gather in Atlanta for that race, Kulwicki had been cajoled by his public relations man, Tom Roberts, to come to town a day early to do interviews with newspaper, radio, and television outlets in the Atlanta area. It had taken some doing, since Kulwicki felt he needed to be doing last-minute work on his No. 7 Ford instead.

At lunch on that day, Kulwicki and Roberts were going into a Hooters restaurant for a press conference with newspaper writers. Hooters was not only sponsoring the season's final race, but it was also the primary sponsor on Kulwicki's car.

On their way to that lunch-time gathering, Roberts asked Kulwicki a question he'd been needing to ask for days. ESPN, which would be covering the championship banquet at season's end, was planning to put highlights of the champion's year over music for the show, and they'd asked each driver to pick a song he thought might be appropriate. Roberts asked Kulwicki what song he'd like to hear, but Kulwicki gave Roberts no answer. That didn't bother Roberts, since he knew the driver sometimes thought a long time about what he wanted to say.

The luncheon and the rest of the day's activities went well, and that night as Roberts and Kulwicki returned to the hotel where they'd started their day, Kulwicki was about to get out and go inside when he stopped and finally answered Roberts' question.

So after Kulwicki had finished second to Elliott in the Hooters 500 on that Sunday, but had stretched his fuel long enough so that he led the most laps and got five bonus points for doing so, Kulwicki won the championship by a mere 10 points.

And when the time came in December for Kulwicki to come to the stage in New York's Waldorf-Astoria Hotel to accept the champion's awards, the music that played was the only song that really ever should have been considered.

When he was getting out of the car on that night in Atlanta, Kulwicki had turned to Roberts and said, "My Way."

It had been hours since Roberts had asked the question. For a minute, he was confused.

"Huh?" Roberts said.

"The song," Kulwicki said. "For the banquet. 'My Way.'"

"Oh," Roberts said, with the light going on in his head. "Okay."

"Yes," Kulwicki said. "'My Way.' But the Frank Sinatra version. It has to be Sinatra." —D.P.

chapter 11

No. 3,
but One of a Kind

*Dale Earnhardt and Junior
before Rolex 24 Hours of Daytona*

In many ways Dale Earnhardt's life and career was the very embodiment of stock car racing.

He grew up watching his father, Ralph, drive on dirt tracks across the Southeast, making a living by battling fender to fender for lap after lap, trying to keep food on the table.

Earnhardt scratched and clawed his way into the sport, too, borrowing money on Fridays to buy tires to race with on Saturday night, knowing that if he didn't win enough money he couldn't pay back the money he'd borrowed.

He won rookie of the year honors in 1979 and, the next year, won a Winston Cup championship. From the time he and team owner Richard Childress hooked up for good in 1984 and started running the No. 3 car, Earnhardt's legend just kept growing.

To start looking back at Earnhardt's career, we begin with a story Jim McLaurin wrote for *The State* in Columbia, South Carolina, on November 13, 1994, after Earnhardt won his seventh Cup title.

The Fast Lane: Earnhardt Finds Fame a Constant Burden

There is something robot-like in Dale Earnhardt as he goes about his life as the world's greatest race car driver.

It is almost as if he is a great Shakespearean actor, delivering Hamlet's soliloquy with such apparent fervor that women in the audience swoon and grown men reach for their handkerchiefs—all the while thinking, "If I don't get out of these tights soon, I'm going to pass out."

Whether it's signing autographs even as he's carrying on a conversation with someone else, or walking within a phalanx of security guards while his adoring fans reach out just to touch him, something in Earnhardt's demeanor tells you that sometimes his mind and his body are not in the same place.

Even in moments of joy, there is a part of the man that he keeps to one corner of a private little room within himself. No one is invited in.

But, sometimes, the door opens just a crack.

Earnhardt was enjoying the post-race, post-championship banter with the press after his win in the ACDelco 500 in Rockingham—which also locked up his seventh Winston Cup championship—saying all the right things, getting the appropriate laughs, when the question came from out of the blue:

"Dale," a reporter asked, "after the accident in February, did you ever feel like you might not be emotionally ready to do what you needed to do to win the championship?"

"What?" Earnhardt asked, not quite comprehending the question.

"After Neil Bonnett's accident," the reporter said.

There was a long pause. Earnhardt dropped his head slightly, shielding his eyes under the bill of the ever-present baseball cap.

"I'd rather not elaborate on that," he said, then paused again. When he looked up, there was genuine pain in his face. His voice was halting when he spoke: "I can't go fishing in my own lake because of Neil," he said. "Because we fished in it all the time. I can't....I've tried....It's Neil's pond."

There was a rare silence in the press box. Earnhardt, in a most simple way, had shown us the grief he still carried over the loss of the best friend, to whom he'd dedicated his championship.

In those fleeting moments, we had gotten a peek inside that tiny room. We would not be allowed to stay. Earnhardt gently but firmly closed the door.

"Here," he said, with mock gruffness, reaching over to grab the microphone from the moderator. "It's my championship, ain't it?"—meaning, let's move on.

The expected laugh came.

The tension was broken, and there was an embarrassed relief on both sides; Earnhardt, for having let us inside, and the reporters, for having seen—if only for a flicker—an intensely personal side of a very private man.

There is an almost mystical aura about Earnhardt, that somehow the racing gods reached down and endowed him at birth with superhuman qualities; that he just "happened."

But that's not so. His only gift, if you can call it that, was being born in the right place at the right time.

"I could rattle 'em off," he said. "From Ned Jarrett to Tiny Lund to Humpy Wheeler to Richard Howard—the Pearsons, the Pettys, the Yarboroughs—everybody has made me a better racer.

"People say I'm from the old school: 'He's aggressive. He races harder than he should sometimes.' But I learned from the guys who raced like that."

If there's one thing Earnhardt understands, it's where he came from, and the people who helped him get to where he is.

"I tell you," Earnhardt said, "I've been fortunate to, one, have had a great life as a kid growing up around a racing family and a dad that raced, and then having great friends in racing that helped me along when I started racing.

"Guys from Richard Petty on down have helped me. The Allisons, David Pearson, everybody. Tiny Lund, I had some great sportsman races with him at Hickory Speedway and places like that. Bobby Isaac…I could name guys that got me going in this sport, and it's carried me to where I am today. I've learned from the best. I learned from the legends."

There's no insincerity, then, when Earnhardt says he will never replace Petty as the king of stock car racing, nor false humility.

Petty, Earnhardt says, has done things for the sport that no man ever has nor ever will. Not just the 200 victories that will likely never be surpassed, nor the seven championships, which Earnhardt has equaled.

Petty made racing respectable, and racers respected.

"I just tried to put it out of my mind of tying Richard Petty's record," Earnhardt said. "I knew what it would mean. It would mean a lot to me, and I'm proud and honored to be in the same group, as far as being tied with him.

"But he's still the king. He's done it all. He pioneered it and got us to where we are today. I can't take that away from him; I don't care how much I win or what I do."

Dale Earnhardt lives in a world of big money, fast cars, and life-in-the-balance decisions made in the blink of an eye. It is a world of smoke and noise and danger and bravery and sometimes tragedy.

His skill has made him wealthy beyond his wildest dreams, and an object of the kind of adulation that must seem strange to a simple man who grew up with no other ambition than to drive a race car.

It is a world that makes big heroes. And right now, love him or hate him, Earnhardt is the biggest.

But fame carries a heavy price. He is tugged at constantly from all directions; an autograph here, a public appearance there, a sponsorship commitment halfway across the country—all at the same time.

"I tell you," he said, "it beats you down, with all the ways people pull on you for time or whatever it may be. It's all part of the game, and it's gotten more and bigger and bigger."

Earnhardt is not comfortable being an idol. In one breath he says that he loves his fans, and he's sincere. In the next, the constant adulation is "a big part of my life that I don't really enjoy, but you've just got to smile and say yes or okay or sign that autograph or whatever."

Time is a racer's most important commodity, whether it's the thousandths of a second he can shave off of a lap, or the few hours he can get away from the clamor. Of the latter, he says, there is precious little.

"It's unbelievable," he said. "If you could follow me around for a day, it would probably amaze you.

"Sometimes about 3:00 in the afternoon I'm about ready to blow my brains out. On a Tuesday or a Wednesday, when you're trying to straighten out everything that's going on and where you're going and what's happening.

"I sign autographs, on average, an hour and a half every day in the office, and I'm still a week behind, and it's piling up. The fan response is great. That's the part you do and love; everything's part of the job.

"I've learned a lot about it, though. I'm learning every day how to handle it. I wasn't too good at it in '79 and '80, but I've learned to smile a little bit."

On the Wednesday before the ACDelco 500, Earnhardt had finished a press conference and stood in a small hallway chatting with a few friends. Perhaps unwittingly, he said something that goes a long way in explaining why, at times, he seems to be on remote control.

"I make a lot of phone calls that nobody knows about," Earnhardt said. "To sick people; to kids who are dying.

"I called the preacher the other day and asked him to come out to the farm. We rode off over on a back corner and had a long talk. I asked him, 'What do you say to people like that? How do you handle it?'...

"I can send them autographed caps or pictures or call them on the phone," he said. "But sometimes people want things out of Dale Earnhardt that he just can't deliver." —J.M.

I'm Sorry, Ed

Ed Clark, the boss at Atlanta Motor Speedway, was having trouble with Dale Earnhardt. Big deal. Move over, and join the club. Apparently a lot of people had trouble with Earnhardt.

"One of my favorite Earnhardt stories was when we built the condos at the speedway," Clark said. "Dale got a condo and we gave him a deal on it, and in return he'd do appearances for us. He did the first one. The next one I asked him to do was to come to a children's charity dinner. I wrote him a letter and sent it to Don Hawk, who was his business manager, and never got a response."

Clark was pretty close to Earnhardt—they did a lot of things together—so he called Don Hawk, who told him he'd have to ask Dale. He still didn't get a response, so he left Hawk a terse message and got a reply saying that Dale was Ed's friend, and he'd handle it.

"So that was the week of the Homestead race. That was when [Atlanta] ran the last race," Clark said. "It was the last Nationwide race, and it was Dale's assistant, and she said, 'Are you coming to Homestead? He'll get with you at the race.' I said, 'Yeah, I'll be there Sunday.'"

Clark never saw Earnhardt at Homestead, and the Atlanta track was holding a condo owners meeting the next Friday.

"In the middle of the meeting I look out the window, and a black Trailblazer pulls up," Clark said. "Out comes Earnhardt with a laundry bag and a driver's suit in it. And he walks in and says, 'Would you guys take a break? I need to talk to Ed.' We go back in the little kitchen area and he says, 'Don't be mad at Hawk. If you're going to be mad at somebody, be mad at me.' So I said, 'I am. I'm mad at you.' And he says, 'I guess I got it coming.'"

So Earnhardt gave Clark the driver's suit in lieu of attending the charity dinner, and he promised to help Clark for Atlanta's next race. And he asked Clark not to be mad at him.

"He could dish it out, but he couldn't stand if you were mad at him," Clark said. "He ended up winning the race, and we're in victory lane, and we're standing there, and he says 'Don't forget. Anything you want next time, but you gotta give me some time. Don't call the day before.'

"About three different times he said something to me, trying to make up for me being mad at him. That's kind of the way he was. He had a sensitive side that people didn't see. But it was there, and it was obvious if you knew him well. That really bothered him that I was truly ticked off at him."

Earnhardt's last win at Atlanta came March 12, 2000, in the Cracker Barrel 500.

But Clark also remembers visiting Earnhardt early in Dale's career. It could have been after his rookie of the year season in 1979 or his first championship year, 1980.

Clark visited Earnhardt's house on a Sunday afternoon, and Dale's crew chief and a bunch of other people were there. Most of them were waterskiing.

"It was the first time I ever saw one of those tube things you pull behind a boat. And they were out there doing stupid things. Earnhardt asked—I won't use the words he said—but basically he was asking if I was afraid to get on it. I said I've been watching, and I'm not sure I'm up for it. He gave me a bunch of crap, and he said, 'I tell you what, I'll drive the boat, I'll go slow. Just get back then and ride the thing and play around a bit, and it'll be fine.'

"And, of course, I was dumb enough to believe that."

Earnhardt was waving at Clark, and everything was fine. They went into a cove and had to turn around, so, naturally, Earnhardt ran the motor wide open, and Clark made a wide arc and came about three feet off the water. Finally, the boat came around and Clark came back down.

Unfortunately, "I hit a wave of water about five feet high, the wave from where he came in," Clark said. "I probably went 30 feet in the air and landed on the back of my neck. It just really just stunned me. I was laying in the water, and it scared the bejesus out of Earnhardt. He turned the boat around and pulled me in, saying how sorry he was. I was so mad, I could have killed him, if I'd had a stick.

"But that was his way. He couldn't not do it. He *had* to do that."—T.G.

A "Goll-eee" Moment

It is difficult for race fans today to think of Dale Earnhardt in any other terms than as "the Intimidator."

But there was a time when Earnhardt was young and impressionable, and nowhere was that more evident than when he and his buddies went to Daytona to race for the first time in 1976.

Earnhardt and his brothers Danny and Randy, along with long-time crew chief and lifelong friend Tony Eury, Rick Bost, and Mike Bostick, who would later become Earnhardt's brother-in-law, loaded his late-model sportsman race car and all packed into an old beat-up one-ton Chevy truck and headed for the beach.

"It was my dad's truck, and we put a case of oil on the back when we left home," Earnhardt recalled in an interview in 1998. "When we got back, we didn't have a can left. Every time we'd stop for gas, we'd put in two quarts of oil. She was a pretty wore-out truck."

Earnhardt said that his first impression of the track as they exited I-95 onto Volusia Boulevard in Daytona was not intimidating, but even he had to gulp.

"We saw the end of the race track and kept driving by, kept driving by, and I said, 'Oh Lord, how big is this thing?'" he said. "You see pictures of it, and see it on TV, but you never realize how big this place is. That was a pretty awesome deal right there, driving by the place, then the next morning when we went in for inspection, and it was unbelievable."

Earnhardt qualified 22nd for his first race at Daytona and, he said, "finished 13th with a bad fuel filter. Should have been better."

But there was nothing like the experience.

"I never remember being scared of what was going on," Earnhardt said. "It was like the whole time was unbelievable, and we were just having a big time the whole time.

"I'd be walking around and there would go Richard Petty, and here would go David Pearson. What time I wasn't on the track, I was watching them, watching around the Winston Cup garage. It was something else."

But, even then, he had a little bit of the Intimidator in him.

"Turn off your tape recorder," he said, "and I'll tell you about the night life." —J.M.

Back It Up

Jay Wells was a publicist for North Carolina Motor Speedway in Rockingham when he took a temporary assignment with Charlotte Motor Speedway in the early 1980s. They needed a temporary publicist for the Coca-Cola 600, and Wells volunteered.

The problem was that Wells couldn't afford to keep up his home in the Rockingham area *and* a hotel room in the Charlotte area. So Joe Whitlock, then the chief publicist at CMS, introduced Wells to Earnhardt, who said that Wells could stay in his basement. When visitors would show up, Wells might poke his head out, and Earnhardt would say that Wells was the troll who guarded his bridge. So the 5'6" Wells was stuck with a nickname for life: the Troll.

It got worse later, though, when he was working the Skoal Bandit account for U.S. Tobacco. He showed up somewhere one day, and someone (not Earnhardt) said, "It's the Troll from Skoal—the Skoal Troll!"

"I wore [the nickname] like a badge of honor," Wells said. "Everybody kinda had a nickname of their own, [and I had] the Troll, the Skoal Troll. And it still lives with me to this day. I haven't worked with U.S. Tobacco since 1995. It's been 12 years, and people still say, "Come here, Skoal Troll."

Most people have a crazy Earnhardt story. Wells can go them one better with a story about Earnhardt driving a car backward. Relax, though; apparently he didn't put a rear bumper to another guy's rear bumper, and no one was turned into the wall.

"I can honestly say that he had a true sixth sense about what was in front of him, in back of him, from side to side," Wells said.

Earnhardt and Wells went to a barbecue in Mooresville, North Carolina, then headed to Earnhardt's race shop in Kannapolis, about 14 miles away.

"We'd been drinking Jack Daniel's, and Earnhardt had a Pontiac Trans Am, like Smokey and the Bandit," Wells recalled. "He started smoking the tires, but then the transmission locked up. What do we do? What do we do? How are we going to get home? He said, 'Hold on,' and he started driving from Mooresville backward! It was about 11:00, and Cannon Mills was having a shift change.

"Earnhardt said, 'This guy's going too slow,' and he'd pass him! Going backward, he'd pass a car. He'd come up behind another one, and he'd say, 'Hold on!', and he'd pass another one. I turned the bottle straight up; I was about 24 years old at that point."

You have to wonder how Earnhardt could see to drive; his headlights were heading the wrong way.

Wells says that Earnhardt got nervous and began worrying about a highway patrolman catching his act. So he parked the Pontiac for about a half hour.

"Then we started again and went backward through downtown at 12:00 or 12:30," Wells said. "It was about 14 miles."

Wells paused as he thought about the memory.

"He had the ability to do amazing things," he said. —T.G. (*Angel in Black: Remembering Dale Earnhardt Sr.*)

Over? Who Says It's Over?

At times, it looked as if Dale Earnhardt was inventing new ways to lose the Daytona 500. But in none of those races that he lost did he get a bigger roar out of the crowd than in 1997.

Earnhardt and his nemesis, Jeff Gordon, were battling for second place while chasing down leader Bill Elliott with 11 laps to go when they came off the second turn side-by-side.

Earnhardt's car carried to the outside wall, and when he bounced off it, he tagged Gordon, then got hit from behind by Dale Jarrett. His black GM Goodwrench Chevrolet went back into the wall and flipped onto its roof, then slid down the backstretch before it flipped onto its wheels in the grass.

The fans in the frontstretch who had seen the tumble on the giant TV screen could not believe what they saw next. Even as the caution flag was still flying, Earnhardt came tearing around the Turn 4 apron in the badly damaged car, setting off a roar that drowned out the engines of the race cars.

After Earnhardt had climbed out of the car, he walked to the ambulance and then walked back to the wreck, which was being hooked to the tow truck.

"I looked at the wheels and told the guy in the car to fire it up," Earnhardt said. "It fired up and I said, 'Get out! Unhook me! I've got to go!'"

His dream of winning the big one was on hold for another year, but Earnhardt didn't cast any blame on Gordon.

"After it was all over," Gordon said, "I saw this mangled black No. 3 car coming and I said, 'Uh-oh.' But he came by and gave me a thumbs up. To me, that was an okay, that he wasn't putting any blame on my side."

Earnhardt and his crew's heroic efforts to pound his car into good enough shape to finish the race turned out to be largely symbolic because he would have dropped only one spot in the finishing order. But the fact that they did said a lot about why—and how—Earnhardt won seven Winston Cup titles.

"We took off after 'em," Earnhardt said. "You've got to get every lap you can. That's what we're running for the championship for." —J.M.

A Sure Thing for a Dream

What would make a man who has reached the top of his profession chuck it all to pursue a dream? For Kirk Shelmerdine, the dream was reason enough.

Shelmerdine, who went South from Pennsylvania in 1981 to chase his dream to be a Winston Cup driver, saw his road take a detour (almost) when he passed the Mason-Dixon Line. Instead of becoming a driver, he became one of the most successful mechanics the sport of auto racing had ever seen.

"When I was a teenager and moved down here, I wanted to be a driver," Shelmerdine said. "That was my motivation for getting into racing. I always had that kind of desire in me. I was wired for it. But the opportunities never represented themselves in such a way that that was my best move to do so.

"I got involved in the mechanical end, and that lasted an awful long time. I saw an awful lot of success there."

Success indeed.

After two years of being a one-man crew for independent driver James Hylton, Shelmerdine signed on with a young owner-driver named Richard Childress and in doing so, hitched his wagon to a star.

Childress re-signed a driver he couldn't afford a couple of years earlier, and the threesome made history. Dale Earnhardt became the most successful driver of the 1980s and 1990s, winning six of his seven championships from 1986 to 1994, and Shelmerdine was the man under the hood for four of those titles.

As the crew chief on Earnhardt's No. 3 Chevrolets, he became the youngest crew chief to win a Winston Cup race, at 25 in 1983, and at 28, he became the youngest to win a Winston Cup championship. At 29, he was inducted into the International Mechanics Hall of Fame.

Clearly, Shelmerdine was cut from special cloth, and the combination of Earnhardt, Childress, and himself could have won more titles. (Earnhardt won his sixth and seventh in 1993 and 1994, after Shelmerdine left.) In fact, had he stayed, they probably would have broken Earnhardt's and Richard Petty's shared record of seven championships.

But as good as he was at it, being a mechanic was, in the end, just a job. Driving a race car, the dream he'd put on hold in 1981, was his passion.

So with the world on a string, he cut that string, said good-bye to the big money, and basically started over. He opened his own little shop in Welcome, North Carolina, right down the street from Childress.

With an annual budget that would not have covered the expenses of one race with his old team, Shelmerdine would never again enjoy the success he had as a crew chief, but he found happiness instead.

"Someday I'll put all my 101 reasons in a book," he said, "but for now, I'll say it got old, I guess. I was burned out. Totally.

"It wasn't one main straw that broke the camel's back; it was a combination of things. I put all the pros and cons together and presented them to myself in a clear way, and the cons clearly outweighed the pros. I had to go. There was no use to try to Band-Aid it or go ask the boss for more money or look for some other reason to do it. If you're not happy and not able to give 100 percent, you shouldn't be doing it."

Shelmerdine loved the driving but couldn't pay the bills, so he hired himself out as a "consultant" from time to time, and even had offers from team owners to be a combination driver–crew chief, but he was not so dumb that he couldn't see that all they wanted was his mechanical skills, not his driving ones.

"In 1994 and '95, I took a Busch (Series) ride that was supposed to be full-time, with sponsorship and stuff, and the second time I even came up with the sponsorship," he said. "I went to the car owner, he took all the money, bought a new tractor-trailer, and fired me after the first seven races....I wanted the driving thing to blossom into something probably a little bit too badly."

He has enjoyed what could generously be called "modest success" as a driver, racing in minor-league circuits all over the country, and by 2005 he had worked himself into a position where he was making a full-time attempt at the Nextel Cup circuit, though without much success.

He may one day change his mind and take a crew chief's job again, but it would not be because it's what he wants. Even if another wealthy team owner such as Rick Hendrick came along and offered him the moon, he'd be hard-pressed to take it.

"In the first place, he wouldn't do that," Shelmerdine said. "Second, I don't know if I could actually justify it. What have I got to gain? I've already won enough of those [championship] belt buckles to last a while. Forty-six races. What is there for me to shoot at? Driving presented that for me. It was kind of a lofty goal that got my enthusiasm going again.

"It is all the same old BS I've been doing for years, but from a whole new perspective.

"Looking through the windshield is different. It presented me a whole new ladder to climb." —J.M.

Bumped and Handcuffed

Geoff Bodine may joke about it now, more than 20 years later, but his battles with Dale Earnhardt were no laughing matter in the 1980s and '90s. Some people described their battles as North vs. South or a new Civil War, Iron Head's rebel vs. Geoff's Yankee.

Who'd crack first? Bodine? No, wouldn't happen. Earnhardt? Are you kidding? NASCAR? Definitely not. So something was about to explode.

At least one incident from the Bodine-Earnhardt feud—the two rental cars—was used in the 1990 movie *Days of Thunder*. That's not exactly what happened—they only had one rental car. Dale, in the passenger's seat, was urging Geoff to bump the car in front with NASCAR boss Bill France Jr. in it, but he didn't. No one got wrecked when they met with France, but that's Hollywood for you.

In 2007, Bodine recalled one of the biggest feuds of NASCAR's Winston Cup era (1971–2003):

"Dale started the bump and run, and I started the penalty box, because he bumped me, and I bumped him, and I got in trouble," Bodine said with a laugh. "It took me a while to figure out that that wasn't working. He'd get away with it, and I'd get in trouble. We kept doing it. [Car owner] Rick Hendrick got upset with Dale running into his cars all the time, causing us trouble, and he said [to me], 'Look, if you don't figure out a way to stop this, I'm going to find another driver who will.' He put the pressure on me to do something, to figure out how to get Dale into trouble, and that's what happened at Charlotte that weekend before the meeting [with France]."

Earnhardt spun Geoff out that week in the Busch race. He didn't get Dale back that day. He waited.

"I'm not real smart," Bodine said, "but I try not to be stupid. In Sunday's race, I hit him first. I didn't wreck him; I just got him a little sideways. That made him mad, and we went into Turn 3, and he just put me straight into the wall. And that's when Bill Jr. called us all up that night—he actually called [car owners] Rick Hendrick and Richard Childress up—and said to get your drivers down here, we're going to have a meeting."

At the meeting, France showed the drivers video of the two races, and France put down his foot...on their heads.

"He told us both, 'Look, this is NASCAR, this is how I make my living, and you're messing with the way I make my living, and I don't appreciate it. I'm going to tell you guys how you're going to act from here on out,'" Bodine said. "He told us he didn't want bumping anymore, he didn't want to see us near each other. He said, 'I don't want to see you guys on the same track. If you get close, I'll have to bring you in [the pits] and make sure your steering's right. And if you touch, if you bump, the consequences are going to be pretty steep.'"

So for the rest of that year, Dale and Geoff stayed away from each other.

But the ceasefire didn't last.

Around 1992, they were racing at Bristol. The late Alan Kulwicki was leading; Bodine was second, and Earnhardt was a lap down after a flat tire.

"So he was coming up through the pack, and he got to me, and I raced him for a couple laps," Bodine said. "I thought, 'What am I racing him for? Let Alan race him for a while; let Alan hold him back.' So I moved up the track and motioned him by, and he spun me out for no reason. Back then, people had scanners; scanners were starting to come in, and everyone was listening. [Car owner Richard] Childress said, 'What happened?' Earnhardt said, 'Ah, Bodine was in my way; I just put him out.'

"He admitted right on the radio what he'd done. And that was the first time since the meeting in Daytona that he did anything. Up until then, he didn't bump-and-run me. That day, for some reason, he just felt like turning me around, for no reason, because I'd moved out of his way."

Bodine says that Earnhardt's car owner then, Bud Moore, asked Earnhardt why he did it and didn't get an answer.

"That was totally wrong, but that was Dale," Bodine said. "But he did that to everybody; it wasn't just me. If you didn't get way out of his way, he'd bump you and turn you around. He thought it was supposed to be that way."

And Earnhardt occasionally got his way off the track, too. Geoff still seems uncomfortable as he remembers the incident with Dale and the handcuffs…yes, handcuffs. It's an arresting story.

Bodine says they were at the old track in Louisville, Kentucky, and were doing media interviews before the weekend of racing. They went out on the balcony to the tiny media center, and Earnhardt got rambunctious.

"We walked out on a balcony they had, and he grabbed some handcuffs from a security guard and walked to me when I wasn't looking and put one end to my hand and one end to the railing," Bodine says with lingering disgust. "He started laughing; of course *everybody* started laughing except me. That made me pretty upset. It was kinda embarrassing, number one, and number two, I have a little claustrophobia. I didn't feel comfortable being chained, handcuffed to that railing. Immediately, I said, 'Hey, get these things off me.'

"He didn't do it right away. I said, 'Listen, get these things off me right now.' He was chuckling, and they could see I was pretty upset, so everyone kinda stood back to see what happened. He eventually uncuffed me, obviously. But that started a war that night for the race. In the heat race, he tried to spin me out, and in the feature race he tried to spin me out. That was a fun night. The race fans got a good show out of that one."

Few relationships were cut-and-dried with Earnhardt.

"We started out as friends," Bodine said. "When I first moved down [from Chemung, New York, to North Carolina], we went to dinner with him. My kids and their mother stayed there at the lake for a weekend and had a good time.... We actually rode some horses with him. [My brother] Todd had a horse farm. We were over there one time, and I had a couple horses. He and Dale Jr.—it was quite a while ago, Dale Jr. was just a little guy—we rode some horses together.

"Away from the track, we weren't buddies, but we respected each other. At the track, it was a different situation. It was competition, and Dale didn't like to get beat."

Off the track, "He'd come behind you and grab you," Bodine recalled. "That was his signature, I guess, to come up from behind, put his arm around you, and put the choke hold on you. Or else grab you by the shoulder and squeeze; he was a pretty tough guy. It was fun. What I read from that was that he cared, he respected you, he wasn't trying to hurt you. But we never hung out; we were never buddy-buddy after the first year or two. He knew his limits. You learn your limits with people."

Even Earnhardt, a man who raced to the limit and beyond, had limits. They were just far out. —T.G. (*Stock Car Magazine*)

A Penny for Your Thoughts

When Tony Stewart started climbing fences after winning races during the 2005 season, it was another take on victory celebrations that have always been a part of the story in NASCAR.

Alan Kulwicki, the driver-owner who shocked the stock car racing world in 1992 by winning the championship, was known for his "Polish victory lap." Kulwicki wanted to see the fans cheering him when he went around the track after a win, so he turned around and went clockwise on an oval with the driver's side toward the grandstands.

The crowd loved it, but NASCAR wasn't so thrilled. Afraid that other cars or track safety vehicles might not be expecting Kulwicki to be coming the "wrong" way, he was "urged" by NASCAR not to make a habit of doing the reverse lap. He promised he wouldn't do it again until he won the Daytona 500 or the championship, so after he finished second in the Hooters 500 at Atlanta Motor Speedway in 1992, edging Bill Elliott for the championship, Kulwicki broke it out again.

Drivers have done various versions of burnouts and doughnuts over the years.

Kyle Busch, after winning a Busch race at Charlotte, spun his tires to create a cloud of smoke and then climbed out of his car so he could be there, standing on the window sill to salute the fans, when the smokescreen dissipated.

Two of the most famous post-race celebrations came after veteran stars got their first Daytona 500 victories after years and years of trying. Darrell Waltrip had failed to win the sport's biggest race in 17 tries, but in 1989 he and crew chief Jeff

Hammond saw opportunity present itself. Waltrip stayed on the track and stretched his final load of fuel for more that 130 miles.

And won the Daytona 500.

"This is Daytona isn't it?" Waltrip asked in victory lane. "Don't lie to me! Don't tell me I am dreaming!"

Waltrip then did his version of the "Icky shuffle," mimicking—quite poorly—the end-zone dance done by Cincinnati Bengals football player Icky Woods, "spiking" his driver's helmet in the process.

Nine years later, history would repeat itself when another long-time superstar ended a career filled with Daytona 500 frustration by winning the race in his 20th try.

Earnhardt was leading the final lap in 1990 when he had a flat tire going into Turn 3, and Derrike Cope went by him to win. In 1993 Dale Jarrett had passed Earnhardt in the final laps on his way to winning the 500.

Finally, in 1998, Earnhardt got to the checkers first. He took a long, slow lap around the track and then, as he came off Turn 4 and headed down pit road, crews from virtually every team in the sport were lined up to congratulate him. It was an amazing sight, a tribute to one of NASCAR's all-time best.

When Earnhardt had slapped the last high-five, he gunned the engine of his black No. 3 Chevrolet and looped it twice in the infield grass. It wasn't until later, after the excitement of the moment died down, that people began to realize that the mark Earnhardt had left in the grass looked very much like the number "3." Could he have possibly done that on purpose?

More than an hour after that race, with Earnhardt high above the track in the press box doing the winner's interview

he'd always wanted to do, fans began doing the strangest
thing. Carrying their coolers and souvenir bags they'd had with
them all day, a few of them went into the infield grass and
began picking up chunks of grass from where Earnhardt had
made his mark.

There are all kinds of great stories about how Earnhardt
celebrated that night. Hours later, ESPN was on the air doing
a late *SportsCenter*, and Earnhardt was seen riding past their
broadcast position on the back of a security guard's
motorcycle. Much, much later, he was down on the beach with
some friends toasting the victory with the trophy still in his
hands.

At 4:30 PM Sunday afternoon, about an hour after the
Daytona 500 ended, the first fan got in line to be one of 180 to
be admitted into a question-and-answer session at Daytona
USA, which would follow the ceremony where the race-winning
car was put on display for a year in the museum. More than two
dozen fans spent the night in line, sitting through a driving rain.
The line for seats was cut off at 7:30 the next morning.

"Race fans are pretty special people," Earnhardt said. "I
have signed autographs where people have had to stand in
line out in the rain and they said, 'I wouldn't have stood in line
for Elvis, but I stood in line for you.'"

It was at that Monday morning ceremony when Earnhardt
told reporters about a little girl he'd met on the day before his
big victory. She was one of five children from the Make-A-Wish
Foundation that Earnhardt met on that Saturday.

"She was rubbing this penny, a brand new one, and she
gave it to me," Earnhardt said. "She said, 'I've rubbed this penny
and it's going to help you win the Daytona 500. It's your race.'"

The next day, Earnhardt glued the penny to the dashboard of his car. And for the next year, that penny stayed glued to that dashboard there at Daytona USA.

"For a little girl like that in a wheelchair, who life hasn't been so good to, for her to give me a penny for good luck in the Daytona 500, that's pretty special," Earnhardt said.

It certainly was. —D.P.

Here's $5,000; Come See Us

Eddie Gossage, the long-time president of Texas Motor Speedway, had a problem. They'd just built the track near Fort Worth in 1996, and they wanted to bring some Winston Cup drivers down to promote the place.

Gossage needed something to bait his hook.

"I guess it goes back to when we were building the place, trying to figure out how to get top drivers to tour the construction and get them to help us promote and market, that kind of thing," he said. "I went to Martinsville and gave out invitations to the wives of the drivers in the top 10 in points. The invitation said, 'If you'll come to Texas, we're going to take you for a day of shopping at Neiman-Marcus with a personal shopper assigned to you. Here's a $5,000 gift certificate, but it can only be used that day.'

"Eight of 10 drivers came," Gossage continued. "[Dale] Earnhardt comes to me and says, 'You're sorry,' and I said, 'Why's that?' He said, 'You give [Dale's wife] Teresa $5,000 to get me for a day and a half. I charge $15,000 an hour.' I said, 'I know.'"

Earnhardt wound up having a big time. He got on a
bulldozer and moved some dirt around. He wanted to know
where victory lane was; then he ran over to it because he
wanted to be the first person in victory lane. Dale probably was
the darling of most everyone in Texas for a day or more,
everyone other than possibly Gossage.

They had a dinner for the drivers and wives at Ross Perot
Jr.'s ranch. Ross Perot Sr. was there, as were golfer Freddy
Couples and former Cowboys coach Tom Landry. The track
spent $40,000 on the gift certificates, since only eight of the
10 drivers showed up.

"They were here for a day and a half, which was their
complaint," Gossage said. "It was cheap compared to what it
would cost to get those guys here otherwise.

"The wives had a big time. We had lunch and a fashion
show lined up for them at Neiman-Marcus. They went
shopping, and the guys had to be with me and [track owner]
Bruton [Smith] for a day and a half of looking at the racetrack
and looking at the plans. [The drivers] were not thrilled for us,
but we got tons of media coverage out of it, quite a bit deal."

He says it's harder to promote stock car racing in Texas
than it would be in Charlotte, the home of most of the race
teams and the heart of NASCAR country.

"It's always an uphill battle," Gossage said. "As one of the
sports directors told me, if you lead with the Cowboys 365
days a year [in Texas], you're never wrong. The Cowboys can
do no wrong. And I understand that. But we get our share [of
coverage], trust me. We've done real well. Other major-market
speedways will complain to me. They can't get anywhere, no

luck, no success. It can be done; they're just not working it quite right."

Postscript: Earnhardt wasn't the first man in victory lane for a Cup race at Texas; Jeff Burton was, in 1997. Dale Jr. won at Texas in the spring of 2000, but Earnhardt never did. —T.G.

chapter 12

Modern-Day Heroes

Mark Martin crosses finish line first at North Carolina Motor Speedway to win Goodwrench 200, 2-24-96

Sometimes it seems people only tell stories about the guys who're no longer racing. But some of the guys who're still around have had their moments, too.

Unanswered Prayers

In 1995, Dale Jarrett figured his time with Robert Yates Racing was done.

He'd come to the team after Ernie Irvan was seriously injured in a crash a year earlier at Michigan International Speedway, but Irvan had made a miraculous recovery and was nearly ready to return.

That August, Jarrett and his wife, Kelley, were riding in a car with Yates in Indianapolis when Yates said he didn't know if he could make a two-car team work. Jarrett was not surprised by his car owner's position. Multicar teams were not nearly as prevalent in the sport then as they are today. Jarrett knew that it was likely he'd need to have another option when it was time for Irvan to come back.

Jarrett had a sponsor lined up with which he could start his own team. The sponsor had offered more money that Jarrett thought he needed to get a team started. But there was a problem.

Jarrett was a husband and a father—with daughters ages 7 and 5 at the time—and the potential sponsor was Hooters Restaurants, not a particularly good fit.

"Even though it's a very good company, it wouldn't have exactly fit the image that I was trying to portray," Jarrett said. "Making appearances at Hooters wasn't exactly what I wanted to do, and it certainly wasn't what Kelley Jarrett wanted Dale to be doing. But she understood what we had to do. We had to worry about my family and making a living and getting something started."

The contract was on Jarrett's desk, needing only his signature. But Jarrett waited. Several weeks later, Yates decided that he would, indeed, start a second team.

"I realized then and there that's why I hadn't signed that contract," Jarrett said. "There was going to be something there waiting for me. Everybody says God works in mysterious ways. You just don't know. Good things come to those to wait. I waited, and look what happened."

What happened was the No. 88 Ford, the car Jarrett drove to victories in the 1996 Daytona 500, Coca-Cola 600, and Brickyard 400, all within a year of thinking his days with Yates were done. He went on to win the 1999 championship and was driving that No. 88 Ford. —D.P.

With Some Help From Benny and Jeff

It's funny how big-time drivers get noticed.

Jeff Gordon says that he began hearing about Jimmie Johnson when he visited a test at Darlington Raceway and saw Johnson driving a Herzog Motorsports car. In 2000, Johnson drove that entry full time and began to catch the eye of some other team owners.

Gordon went to Darlington to watch Ricky Hendrick, the late son of team owner Rick Hendrick, test in preparation for a Busch (now Nationwide) Series race. As he watched, another driver, Jimmie Johnson, caught his eye.

"I was just standing on top of the truck watching, and I saw a car out there that was running the right line, quick, and looked good, but I didn't recognize anything other than it was a red-and-white [No.] 92 car," Gordon said.

Hendrick hired him and made Gordon the co-owner, and the rest is history. Johnson has one more Cup championship than Gordon.

"I don't even know if I would have had a chance to race in Cup if it wasn't for Rick," Johnson said. "I don't know what he and Jeff both saw in me back in 2000 as I was a mid-pack Busch driver. They saw it, offered me a job. Nobody else was calling offering me a job.

"I don't think I'd be where I am today without Jeff and Rick, what they've put on the line for me."

Greg Biffle, meanwhile, caught the eye of Hall of Famer Benny Parsons during the 1995–96 NASCAR Winter Heat Series, and that led to a pretty good Cup career for Biffle. Parsons told Jack Roush that there was no way he could pass up the chance to hire Biffle, and that if he did he would regret it while watching Biffle win races for someone else.

Biffle became the first driver to become champion in both the NASCAR Nationwide and the Camping World Truck series. He made his first Cup start at California in 2002, and through 2011, Biffle had 330 starts, 16 wins, and nine poles.

He had a personal-best six Cup victories in 2005, and Roush was happy that Parsons spoke up. —T.G. (*Scene Daily*)

Walk Softly, but Keep the Stick Handy

Two-time NASCAR Winston Cup champion Terry Labonte is one of the quietest and most unassuming men in racing, but his calm exterior hides a fierce competitor inside.

When Labonte won the 1995 Goody's 500 at Bristol, he did it by surviving a crash initiated by seven-time champion

Dale Earnhardt at the checkered flag. Labonte didn't raise a big stink, but if it had gone the other way it could have been a different story.

"I won the race, so I'm not mad," Labonte said afterward. "If he had won the race, I might be a little mad. But I don't think he intended to wreck us. We were just both trying to win the race."

But fellow competitor Bobby Hamilton recalled an incident when Labonte was not as forgiving.

"I remember the time that Lake Speed spun Terry out at Bristol," Hamilton said. "They worked on that car and worked on that car. Terry didn't say nothing to nobody. Terry goes back out, wrecks it, pulls back in, and leaves. Terry has a reputation. When you get to Terry, you'd better pass him in a racing-like manner or you're going to get it back. Everybody knows that."

Except maybe one man.

In the 1999 version of the same race at Bristol, Earnhardt did his damage a little earlier, knocking Labonte out of the way on the backstretch on the final lap, going on to take the checkered flag. Earnhardt semi-apologized, saying he only meant to "rattle his cage a little bit," but Labonte came back across his bow with a warning: "He'd better tighten his belts up." —J.M.

They Shot the Truck

Terry Labonte had just captured his second Winston Cup championship, and brother Bobby had just won the season-ending NAPA 500 at Atlanta. Things couldn't be better.

The problem, though, was that he was sitting in the Atlanta Motor Speedway press box, and inquiring sportswriters wanted to know what other interesting things the Brothers Labonte had done together. Terry couldn't think of anything—maybe intentionally—but car owner Rick Hendrick piped in, "What about the truck? You know, you and Bobby shooting the truck?"

The Ice Man began to sweat. His eyes said "How could you?", and he obviously wanted to change subjects. Finally, he gave in.

"Daddy [Bob Labonte] had this truck; it was a piece of junk, and I borrowed it and it broke down on me," Labonte began. "I hated that truck. It broke down on Bobby one day, and he hated it, too.

"My dad called me one day and told us to take it to the junkyard. We called out there to tell them to come pick it up, but I told Bobby, 'You know what? We ought to do something with that truck before they come get it.'

"He said, 'What do you want to do with it?' I said, 'Let's shoot it.'"

So Terry went home, got a .44 magnum, and they killed the truck. Repeatedly.

"Mom comes driving in, and we had one bullet left, and I asked her if she wanted to shoot it," Labonte said with a choked laugh. "She didn't want any part of it."

Good thing. Bob Labonte called home to say he had a buyer for the truck, and he wanted it retrieved from the junkyard. Before they could do anything, their dad went to the junkyard and found the vandalized vehicle.

As the media members laughed, Terry went on:

"Bobby calls me in a panic and says, 'We're in trouble. Dad has sold the truck you shot.' I said, 'You shot it, too,' and he said, 'Yeah, but it was your gun.'"

The argument resembled the TV commercial in which the brothers argued over who's the better driver. And the tongue-lashing by Bob Labonte probably resembled some of the confrontations the Labonte boys faced when they really were boys.

"It took six shots to get it," Terry concluded. "But we got it." —T.G.

Dale Jr. Can't Say Sh*t

Dale Earnhardt Jr. had just won at Talladega Superspeedway and was about to leave the track with the championship lead. Then he stuck his foot in his mouth.

When asked what it meant to have won on the track five times, Earnhardt said, "Well it don't mean sh*t right now. Daddy's done won here 10 times, so I gotta do more winnin'."

Later in the week, NASCAR docked Dale Jr. $10,000 and 100 points, dropping him from the points lead.

A "Can't Say Sh*t" club was instituted, and members of Junior's huge fan base started wearing "Can't Say Sh*t" shirts to various tracks.

Since Junior's verbal faux pas, NBC has instituted a five-second delay for live broadcasts. —T.G.

Sterling's Red-Flag Mishap

Normally, you stop for red lights, red stop signs, and red flags. Sterling Marlin got a little confused in the Daytona 500 back in 2002.

On a late restart, Marlin was trying to pass Jeff Gordon for the lead. They got together, and Gordon spun, causing a multicar crash behind them. Marlin was leading when NASCAR threw the red flag to clean up the mess and finish under green.

With the cars sitting on the backstretch, Marlin exited his car and pulled at his damaged right-front fender. Since you can't touch cars during a red flag, NASCAR sent him to the back.

Ward Burton took the win and probably thanked Sterling afterward. —T.G.

Smiling Like Crazy

Cup driver Clint Bowyer is a funny guy, and he laughs when he remembers his first victory in a Street Stock race in Junction City, Kansas. He was leading the race when a caution came out with five laps left, and the track champion plowed into him, cutting his left-rear tire down.

The crafty move left Bowyer thinking he was done, sitting there with a flat tire. But the track owner let him pit for a new tire and put him back in the lead. Naturally, Bowyer won the race. How else could the story end?

"Well, there was a hell of a fight [afterward]," said Bowyer, who moved from Richard Childress Racing to Michael Waltrip

Racing in 2012. "The fans were fighting; the pits were fighting, and here I was [in victory lane], smiling like crazy with the trophy. So that was my first win. I'll never forget it."

The guy who nailed him probably remembers it, too.

—T.G. (SBNation.com)

Two Sides of the Coin

Ricky Craven has seen both sides of what racing can bring.

He worked his way up through the NASCAR ranks and got a ride with Hendrick Motorsports, one of the most accomplished teams in the Cup Series. But after finishing third in the 1997 Daytona 500 and fifth in the next race at Rockingham, Craven suffered a concussion, a broken shoulder blade, and two broken ribs in a crash at Texas Motor Speedway. He missed two races but returned to run the rest of that season in the No. 25 Chevrolets.

Just four races into the 1998 season, however, Craven admitted that he wasn't 100 percent. He was experiencing headaches and dizziness, and after tests at a hospital he was diagnosed with post-concussion syndrome. He ran four more races for Hendrick Motorsports after returning later that year, but lost the ride he'd worked his whole life to get.

Craven spent the next two seasons trying to convince the garage area that he'd fully recovered. He drove for under-funded teams and did wonders just to get his car into the field most weeks. There were times when he doubted himself, wondered if he'd ever get back in a competitive race car.

But he never gave up.

Late in the 2000 season, as he was trying to convince car owner Cal Wells to let him drive his cars the following year, Craven and his sister, Lauri, opened a store to sell snowmobiles, motorcycles, and all-terrain vehicles in the coastal town of Belfast, Maine, a half-hour's drive from their hometown of Newburgh. The store was across the road from a restaurant where the family used to sit around and eat lobsters on those New England summer evenings that make winter there worth enduring.

Craven knew how much his success in racing meant to the people in that region. So he put up the trophies he'd won in the Busch North and Busch series and the pictures of him with Jeff Gordon and Dale Earnhardt.

Just more than a year later, Craven was able to put another trophy on display in Maine for his fans to see. In the 30th race of the 2001 season, driving the No. 32 Chevrolet owned by Wells, Craven outdueled Dale Jarrett in the final laps to get his first Cup victory at Martinsville Speedway.

Then, in March 2003, Craven and Kurt Busch banged sheet metal all the way down the frontstretch on the final lap of the Dodge 400 at Darlington Raceway. In one of the closest— and best—races in NASCAR history, Craven was ahead at the checkered flag by just two one-thousandths of a second. There has never been a closer finish since NASCAR began using electronic scoring.

When the Cup circuit returned to Darlington later that year for the Southern 500, everybody wanted to talk to Craven about his incredible victory less than six months earlier.

Just after 9:00 AM on race day, only hours before he'd climb back in the car at the track where he'd had the most rewarding moment of his career, the telephone rang in his motor home.

"It's gone," Lauri said, through tears. "It's just gone."

Firemen would eventually surmise that the fire had started near some electrical boxes at the center of the Cravens' store in Belfast, Maine. When the first fire trucks arrived, the fire was already raging. Holes were cut in the roof to vent the intense heat. Lauri arrived and wanted to go inside, hoping she could save something, but firefighters held her back. More volunteer companies showed up to help. Someone knocked in the front door, and the blaze got a fresh gulp of oxygen and flared.

A forklift had been pulled inside for the weekend, and the fire got to it. When its propane fuel tank exploded, the firemen could only pour water to keep the blaze from spreading and had to let the fire burn itself out.

Craven finished eighth in the Southern 500. He honored a commitment to sign autographs at a track in Greenville, South Carolina, the next night. On Tuesday, he went to Maine to see what was left of the place that had been so much more than a family business. It was a place Craven visited often, where he saw his fans and signed autographs and rekindled the strong bond the driver had with those who'd supported him.

Craven didn't get there until around 11:30 PM.

"The very front part of the building was there," he said. "The windows and doors were gone, but I took a flashlight and pointed it in. You couldn't see anything, because there was nothing for the light to reflect off of. It was just black. Imagine a campfire that has burned out. That's what it looked like."

Craven thought it might look better the next morning. There had to be something worth saving. Anything. A trophy, a photograph. Something, But Lauri had been right. It was gone. It was just gone.

Just inside the front door, however, Craven saw something.

It was a coin, a medallion from a box containing one of the No. 32 die-cast cars Craven's fans could buy at the shop. The car was on one side and Craven's signature was on the other.

Somehow, it had survived.

Craven was let go from his Cup ride late in the 2004 season. He drove for Roush Racing in the Craftsman Truck Series in 2005, but the promise that team showed early in the year never played out.

"It takes every ounce of your effort when you're not running well, it just seems like everything is so much harder," Craven said. "But there will be a day when I can think back about having won at every level I've raced and persevering through a lot of stuff."

Craven has kept that coin that survived the fire in 2003. Sometimes he takes it out, looks at it, and wonders why it made it through…and why he found it.

"Some days I look at it and know there are some memories caught up in it," Craven says. "Some days, though, I almost want to get rid of it. People might think it would be a prized possession, but in reality it's almost the reverse of that. I really don't know quite why I've got it or what it represents."

In one regard, though, nothing could be more appropriate.

Trophies remind you of the good times, the days when things lined up and racing seemed easy. Days like March 16, 2003, when Craven barely beat Busch to the finish line in one of the most memorable finishes in NASCAR history.

But nobody knows better than Craven that the bad days—when you shine your light and see only blackness, when things seemingly have been reduced to only a pile of ashes—are ultimately what makes the good ones seem so much better.

The happy times and the hard ones.

Highlights and heartbreaks.

Two sides to a coin. —D.P.

We Were Very Fortunate

Jerry Punch and Rusty Wallace later became co-workers on ESPN's racing programs, but there was a time when Wallace was a big-time race car driver and Punch was an emergency-room doctor.

The two crossed paths many times, most notably in 1988 for the Busch 500 at Bristol Motor Speedway in Tennessee. Rusty was racing, and Jerry was working for Motor Racing Network.

"I had a big old wreck coming off Turn 4 at Bristol, busting my rear end," Wallace has said. "I was kind of laying on a pit wall, knocked out and not breathing and the first guy[s] to the car [were] Dale Earnhardt [Sr.] and Jerry, and Jerry realized what was going on and lifted my head up and got me breathing.

"So I'm glad Jerry was around and I'm glad I'm still working with him. He's really helped me out a lot, that's for sure."

Punch, once a doctor at Halifax Medical Center in Daytona Beach, Florida, said he happened to be in the right place at the right time.

"We were very fortunate," he said. "At that time, Rusty was unconscious and in respiratory arrest. His car was so crumpled from the spiraling—it had somersaulted side over side and end over end—he was obviously unconscious and the roof of the car was compressed.

"We couldn't get to him, and I had just enough fingers to get through the window net to be able to get his jaw pulled forward and get access to the airway and get him breathing from the mouth."

Punch said that Earnhardt stopped on the track, got out of his car, and climbed in the other window of Wallace's car. He said he was screaming at Earnhardt to get someone to take the roof off so we can get to Rusty and help him.

"[I knew] if we could get to him quickly enough and get the airway and get him suctioned out, that he would probably be okay," Punch said. "We were very fortunate."

Punch held Rusty's airway open while NASCAR officials cut the top of the car off with high-speed saws. Punch was sprayed with sparks, and someone held a baseball cap over Punch's face to protect it. They finally got Wallace out, took him to the ambulance, got him awake and alert, and took him to the hospital.

Then Punch returned to work as an announcer. Just when they were ready to go on the air, Wallace called from the hospital, and the feed was funneled through to a production truck and producer Neil Goldberg.

"Wallace said, 'Tell Dr. Punch thank you, but boy, you look terrible' from being covered in soot from the car being cut off and flecks of paint all over," Punch said.

"But we were very lucky that night."

Punch's medical skills helped later that year during an ARCA race in Atlanta. He helped save the life of injured driver Don Marmor, who had no pulse. Punch helped emergency crews stabilize him until a Lifeline helicopter arrived.
—T.G. (*Ventura County Star* and *The Morning Call*)

Viva Las Vegas for Tony Stewart

Chris Powell, the president and general manager of Las Vegas Motor Speedway, says he greatly admires defending Sprint Cup champion Tony Stewart, but he still shakes his head over something that happened around 2006.

"I think it was '06 when we changed the banking on the racetrack," Powell said. "Tony had gotten used to the previous banking and the surface at Las Vegas. We originally paved it in 1996, and it had 10 years to cure. Tony was content the way the surface was."

They increased the banking from 12 degrees to the 20 degrees it is today, and they resurfaced the track.

"Tony had had an opportunity on Friday and early Saturday to go out on the track, but he didn't like the new banking and new surface. The new surface did not have as much grip as the older surface, I don't think.

"I was ambling through the Sprint Cup garage that Saturday. I saw Tony walking from the garage to his transporter and I said, 'Hey, Tony, how do you like the new speedway and the new Neon Garage?' He could not been more direct in his comments, telling me how we'd screwed up a perfectly good racetrack. He told me in no uncertain terms. It was perfectly good, and I'd come along and fouled it up.

"He said, 'We get people who don't know anything racing and they come in here and change things, and drivers are left to deal with the things they've changed.' His index finger may have come in contact with my sternum, my breast bone. It was apparent he was not happy with the new configuration."

Later, TV personality Allen Bestwick was introducing Stewart before the Nationwide race, and Stewart again vented his thoughts on the track.

"Tony called me out by name on national television," Powell said. "It was disconcerting for him to go on national television and express his disappointment with the speedway, a change that we really believed—and I think time has proven it out—that it was going to enhance the racing experience for the race fans."

A tradition of sorts has grown up in Las Vegas. Each year, there's a champions week in which the track takes the current champion for lunch and a question-and-answer session with the local newspaper, the *Las Vegas Review-Journal*.

Stewart, of course, was the 2011 champion, and he got the VIP treatment.

There was a big rectangular table, and Powell was sitting with Stewart.

"It was obvious that, over the years, his feelings had softened because the track has matured and was more to his liking," Powell said. "We're having this lunch and somewhere in there someone asked a question about the behavior of drivers, [since] at the time Kurt and Kyle Busch, Las Vegas natives, were very much in the news about behavioral issues. In his answer about these behavioral issues, he talked about the issues discussing his own behavior, that he himself had had some behavioral issues in the past.

"He said, 'I really got upset with this guy sitting beside me several years ago for his role in changing the speedway here. At the time, I thought I was right. It was the way I felt, but I was wrong in the way I expressed myself. I took Chris to task in a conversation I had with him, and then a few minutes later I made the same remarks on a national TV interview.' He said, 'What I felt at the time, I still believe—that they shouldn't have changed the racetrack, although it is one of the best on the circuit now.

"He said, 'I felt I was right, but I was wrong in the way I expressed myself. I've grown up a lot, and for those of you who don't know, I'm a racing promoter myself.' As you know, he owns Eldora Speedway. He said, 'And I see things from a different perspective today. What the racers believe is not always what a promoter should be believing, and vice versa. There has to be a happy medium. And when one side disagrees with the other, there's a proper way to express that opinion.'

"It was a telling moment to me in that Tony had matured, much like our racing surface. He's one of the most insightful people in the sport. He's been criticized over the years for his temper and some of the things he's said and done, but he's a smart person and has grown up a lot and sees things from a different perspective as a racing promoter himself."

Powell says he doesn't want to hurt Stewart's feelings in retelling the story; he only wants to praise him.

"I don't want this to be negative about Tony," he said, "because I mean it in the most positive way."

Postscript: Just before the 2012 Las Vegas race, Stewart had this to say about the track: "It's no different at Las Vegas than anywhere else [regarding his outlook for the race]. You have to get the car to rotate through the corner, but still stay tight enough on entry and exit. There's no unique challenges there. The track is really smooth and that lets you work on the attitude of your car, and I think that's a luxury that we have there that we don't necessarily always get everywhere else because every track has its unique set of bumps. Vegas has bumps too, but for the most part, it's so smooth that you can really fine-tune the attitude of the car."

Oh, one other thing: Tony Stewart probably likes the Las Vegas track, complaints aside. He got his first 2012 victory at Las Vegas, beating out Jimmie Johnson, Greg Biffle, Ryan Newman, and Carl Edwards. It was Stewart's best finish there. He finished second there in 2000 and 2011, third in 2004, fifth in 2002 and 2003, and seventh in 2007 and 2010. In his first 14 starts at LVMS, he had one win and six top-five and nine top-10 finishes, and he won $2,444,165. —T.G.

Not Too Cool for School

Mark Martin grew up in Batesville, Arkansas, and today he's one of that town's most famous citizens.

He's got a Ford dealership in town now, and he has built a museum there housing as much of the memorabilia from his incredible racing career as he's been able to get his hands on.

Martin has had a lot of great memories in NASCAR. When he won at Kansas Speedway in 2005, it gave him 40 career victories to go with 49 wins in the Busch Nationwide Series. He also won a sixth career championship in the International

Race of Champions Series, the 11th straight time that he's entered that series in which he's finished either first or second.

He's certainly come a long, long way from how things were when he started racing through life in Batesville.

"When I was in high school in Batesville, I felt like I was treated like a strange weirdo," Martin says. "I couldn't play sports—the kind of sports you play in high school—very well. But once I found out that I could race those cars, I knew that's what I wanted to do."

Martin remembers winning the national short-track championship race in Rockford, Illinois, in 1977.

"That was one of the most significant victories of my career, and I was still in high school when I won it," Martin recalls. "I qualified second. Dick Trickle had fast time that day. We did not have the first clue what we were doing and we won the race. It was huge. I still have pictures. I mean, this was a really big deal."

Martin and his father, Julian, jumped in the truck they used to haul Mark's race car and drove all night to get home.

"We got home at 6:00 in the morning," Mark remembers. "I took a shower and went to school. Winning that race was the biggest thing that had happened in my life, but at school that Monday, it was like it didn't happen. That's just the way it was."

After Martin graduated from Batesville High, he and his girlfriend, Arlene, decided to tell Arlene's father they were thinking about a wedding.

"Arlene told her dad, 'I'm going to marry this fellow,'" Martin says. "He said, 'What does he do?' Arlene said, 'He's a race car driver.' Her father said, 'No, what does he do for a living?'"

Now, of course, Martin's father-in-law is one of his biggest fans. The fact that Martin has won more than $50 million in the Cup Series alone has certainly helped that, of course.

Martin started racing when he was just a boy, with his father helping him develop and display his talents. Julian Martin actually started working with Mark long before that. Julian owned a trucking business, and when Mark was barely old enough to stand up in the driver's seat, Julian would let his son steer the truck as Julian controlled the gas and brake pedals.

He'd been racing competitively since 15—he won the third race he ever entered. After every race, Martin would keep a record of how he did and how much money he won. He won a state championship in Arkansas that first year of racing on dirt tracks, and in 1976 moved up to asphalt tracks.

Mark rapidly moved up through the competitive ranks of short-track racing around the Midwest, racing against people sometimes twice or three times his age. He ran against legends like Trickle and Larry Phillips and Larry Shaw. And he did more than hold his own.

Martin won rookie of the year honors in the American Speed Association (ASA) in 1977, then won championships in that series the next three years.

In 1981, Julian and Mark Martin made a foray into NASCAR's top series. Mark, at age 22, made five starts in the Cup Series in 1981—all on short tracks—and never qualified worse than sixth. He won two poles, at Nashville and Richmond, and finished third in his final start that year at Martinsville.

The next season, Martin ran all 30 races and had two top-five finishes, but money promised from sponsors was never delivered. The bills mounted up and, in 1983, he and his father had to auction off their racing equipment to pay them.

Martin eventually returned to the ASA Series for three more seasons, winning another championship in 1986. He tried the NASCAR Busch Series the following year, driving for car owner Butch Lawmaster. Martin's win at Dover that year caught the eye of Jack Roush, a successful sports car racing series owner looking to make his move into NASCAR.

Roush remembers that when he and Martin talked about teaming up, Martin didn't ask about how much money he'd be making or what kind of perks he'd have in his contract. Martin wanted to know about the cars, about who'd be building them and working on them. He knew that if his second chance at NASCAR's top series didn't work out, he'd most likely never get a third.

But, of course, the Martin-Roush pairing did work out. Martin got his first Cup win at Rockingham in late 1989, and he finished third in the championship standings that year. He'd finish sixth or better in the standings 13 times in the next 16 seasons and grow to become one of the most accomplished and respected drivers to ever compete in a NASCAR race.

Just before the 2005 season began in Daytona, Martin invited a group of reporters to his office at a private aviation airport in the Spruce Creek community where he and his family, which includes budding driver Matt Martin, live.

In that office, Martin had built an impressive trophy case that was bulging at the seams with all of the hardware he'd won over the years. He was making plans to get all of those trophies moved to the new museum in Arkansas.

One trophy in the case stood out.

It was from a win in a Cup race at Watkins Glen. Hanging from it on small piece of wire was a lug nut with its threads stripped.

"We should not have won that race," Martin said. "We made a pit stop and put three new tires on; they couldn't change the right rear. We ran that right rear through two stops before we finally got it changed.

"Robin Pemberton, who was changing tires back then wired the nut on there. I walk right up to that and think, 'I remember running two stops and I never dreamed we'd win that race.' But we came back and won. You can look at a lot of those trophies and remember the circumstances involved in winning those races."

That's what the trophies mean to Martin. They're more than just hardware—they represent the stories behind the struggles to succeed.

That's one reason Martin is upset with himself about a decision he made early in his career. He and Arlene were trying to build their lives together, and they wound up moving several times to follow opportunities for Mark to race. Every time they'd move, Mark would pack up the trophies he'd won from the time he was the "oddball" at Batesville High.

One time, finally, Martin decided he wasn't going to move them any more.

"We didn't have a place to put them, and at the time they weren't important to me," Martin said. "Arlene told me it was a bad idea. She said I'd regret it. But I didn't listen."

Years later, Martin saw a trophy that a former rival had kept from a win in an ASA race at the Minnesota state fair. Martin had won that race, too, but he'd discarded the trophy.

"He had that trophy and I looked at that, almost drooling," he said. "I realized, 'Oh my goodness, I don't have one.' I realize now what those meant."

Martin planned to retire from full-time Cup competition after the 2005 season, but Roush asked him to drive the No. 6 Fords for one more year because he needed him.

After 2006, though, Martin said he was determined to step out of the week-after-week grind of the Cup Series. He planned to race in the NASCAR Craftsman Truck Series and run late models at short tracks wherever he felt like that would be fun.

He also kept working on the museum at his dealership in Batesville.

Like a lot of people, whether they're in racing or not, Martin has found that life can be a lot like a race track. Whether you expect to or not, sometimes the finish line winds up being right back where everything started.

"Batesville is place I wanted out of so bad in 1978, I can't tell you," Martin says. "It was way too simple back then for me, but now I long for that simplicity." —D.P.

Buddies from Batesville

Mark Martin had a great little deal going. Carolina Ford Dealers wanted to sponsor him in a Busch Grand National (now the Nationwide Series) stint in 1987.

He even had someone to build the car—his old friend, Bill Davis, from their hometown of Batesville, Arkansas. Great. Wonderful.

But they faced a tiny obstacle, too.

Davis didn't know how to build a race car.

Hey, no problem. Naturally, Martin did the only thing he could do. Martin, who was living in the Greensboro, North Carolina, area, called Davis up in Batesville and told him how to build a Busch car.

Over the phone. No fooling.

"Okay, Bill, now you need to put the sway bar…"

Amazingly, it worked.

"Oh, no, I had never built a race car; I had never been close to one," recalled Davis, who was a Cup car owner from 1993 until 2008.

"I was a mechanically inclined person, of course," Davis added, "but I didn't know how to build a car. So we talked over the phone. I had a list of questions, and he had a list of answers.

"Basically, he told me how to build a race car."

And it was a pretty darned good race car, too. In an era when you didn't have different cars for different tracks, Martin won three races in '87 with car owner Bruce Lawmaster, the ninth one (Dover), the 11th one (Rougemont, North Carolina), and the 22nd one (Richmond).

Then in 1988, Martin and Davis ran only 13 of 30 races. They finished fourth at Daytona in the season opener, won Rockingham in their second race (the third race of the season), and placed seventh at Indianapolis Raceway Park in their sixth race of the year. Martin finished with six top-10s that year. Of course, by then Martin also had a full-time Cup ride with car owner Jack Roush and crew chief Robin Pemberton.

Martin remembers his association with Davis fondly, of course, although he can't tell you how long it took to win with him.

"Not too long, I don't think," Martin said with a modest laugh. "I've had a good go [in the Nationwide Series]."

Which, of course, is an understatement, since Martin's 49 series wins was 18 ahead of the previous record of 31 set by "Iron Man" Jack Ingram.

They ran most of the big races from 1988 to 1990. Martin, who had by then gotten a Winston Cup ride with Jack Roush, took 1991 off from the Busch Series. Then he started up the No. 60 team that has won the bulk of his 49 victories.

Back then, though, it was just natural for them to be together.

Although Davis is eight years older than Martin, they had a lot in common. Davis started out racing motocross, he worked on a top-fuel drag team while in high school, and he drag-raced a street car. Then he joined his father in helping young Mark race stock cars. The Martins and Davises were friends, and Bill worked for Julian Martin, Mark's dad, at his trucking company.

Later, Julian Martin co-signed for Davis to start his own trucking company in Batesville.

In the early 1980s when Martin made a five-race stab at Winston Cup, Davis and Julian Martin drove all over the country to help Martin on his race team. Later, Martin and Davis ran a grand total of six races together, mostly ASA (American Speed Association) and All Pro, before running Busch.

After Martin got his Winston Cup ride with Jack Roush, he made the fateful call to Davis, and their regular collaboration began in earnest.

Gail Davis, Bill's wife, credited Martin for getting Bill into NASCAR.

"A lot of people write about what Bill did for Mark Martin's career, and that's wrong," she said. "It's what Mark did for Bill's career."

Davis agreed.

"We had some great years," Davis said. "We won some races, set some records, sat on some poles, led a lot of laps. We had a lot of success."

They've have had a lot of success since as well. Martin has 40 Cup victories and 49 Busch wins, of course. Davis posted five Cup victories with Ward Burton, including the 2002 Daytona 500, and he later fielded Cup and truck entries for several drivers.

Naturally, Martin and Davis butted heads, as all friends do.

"He'd get so frustrated," Davis said with a laugh. "He'd scream at me that I was wasting his talent. That'd make me madder than hell, of course, and I'd be determined to do better."

Both Martin and Davis, though, remember a falling out they had years later when Davis hired Martin's crew chief, Chris Hussey, away from the No. 6 Roush Racing Cup team.

Eventually, Martin got over his anger. They say they're friends again, although Martin still drives Cup and Davis is out of racing.

There's that connection. When Julian Martin died several years ago in a plane crash, Davis bought the family farm near Batesville. Mark's grandfather, Clyde, stayed on at the farm.

"I loved [the farm], and I didn't want anyone else to have it," Davis said.

After Martin left Davis in 1991, Davis hired Jeff Gordon to drive the No. 1 Baby Ruth Ford.

Davis said he and Martin learned their life lessons from their fathers, but he especially credited Julian Martin for his racing career.

"He taught me how to work," Davis said. "That's all this deal is, hard work. I think Julian taught us never be satisfied, to want more, to achieve more. Mark's one of the most determined, most focused, hardest-working guys I've ever known."

Davis says he's had good associates. His Busch drivers were Martin and Gordon, not a bad pair, and Bobby Labonte, Ward Burton, and Dave Blaney were among his Cup drivers. He also had some good crew chiefs, including Ray Evernham, who paired with Gordon on the Baby Ruth team and later went on to win 47 races and three Cup titles with Gordon and Hendrick Motorsports.

"I've been fortunate with the people I picked," Davis said. "Certainly, I've always prepared good race cars and good people make it all possible. It's been wonderful. Mark taught me to race. The Labontes are good friends, and they helped us.

"It's been a two-way street, though. We've complemented each other."

And they've complimented each other as well.

Martin says he's amazed that he and Davis came so far from Batesville and Julian Martin's trucking company. Still, it doesn't *surprise* him, if that makes sense.

"It doesn't seem any more strange that Bill has come as far as he has any more than myself," Martin said. "It *is* a little bit strange, period.

"Still, I'm not surprised when Bill Davis is successful at anything that he does. I know that; I know him." —T.G.

One Life to Give

It seemed like an ordinary day. Larry Hicks had just come home from his job as a conservation officer and he and wife, Donna, were watching the 6:00 PM news.

Suddenly, they looked out the window and saw Jack Roush's ultra-light plane hit the power lines. Hicks then raced to the porch and saw the tiny airplane floating in the lake beside their house.

He told Donna to call 911, and he jumped in his 14-foot boat and headed out. When he smelled the aviation fuel, he stopped and yelled again: "No matter what happens, I love you."

That frightened Donna, but she dutifully called for emergency help. Hicks, who retired as a U.S. Marine Corps sergeant major in 1990, had to save Roush. He'd taken an air search and rescue course in Japan during some spare time in 1984; the Marines teach people to do, so Hicks did.

He dived in the water and went down once. He didn't find anything, so he came up for air. The second time down, he went to the bottom of the eight feet of water and found nothing; on his way back up, he touched something. It was Roush's neck.

The third time, Hicks brought Roush up with him, then held the wing of the tiny plane with one arm and Roush with the other.

Larry says that Roush was not breathing, then added, "But the Good Lord was not ready to take him."

Hicks performed CPR; on the fifth breath, Roush roused enough to cough up water and blood. Hicks pushed another breath into Roush to make sure. Within 15 minutes, help arrived. On the shore, officers and paramedics washed the aviation fuel off Hicks, and he and Roush were taken to a local hospital.

At that time, Hicks didn't have high hopes for Roush's recovery. Between the drowning and the head and leg injuries, Roush shouldn't have made it.

But that didn't take into account the fighting spirit of Roush, who was celebrating his 60th birthday by flying a friend's plane. Within a few days, Hicks was visiting Roush in the hospital.

"It was extremely emotional," Hicks said. "For the longest time, we couldn't talk.

"I was in the war in Vietnam, a lot of people were killed around me, and I never got a scratch, but this was something totally different. Your life has a positive point, something that you can look back on and say, 'I did something super-special.'"

Hicks didn't care much about NASCAR in the mid-1980s. He was into hunting and fishing, and, in fact, he became an Alabama conservation officer after retiring from a position in public affairs with the Marines.

He had no expectations one day in 1986 or '87—he doesn't remember which—when someone introduced him to another hunter. Fellow named Dale Earnhardt. Seemed like a nice guy. Sure, he was opinionated and he was hard on the other guy, but Hicks came away liking him.

But not enough to root for him. He wasn't a racing kind of guy.

But then Hicks saved Roush, and it all changed. Hicks become a race fan, and most of his favorite drivers drove for Roush.

Hicks, meanwhile, was becoming a celebrity. Roush was making a remarkable recovery, and people were talking about Jack's good fortune. Let's face it—what are the chances that Roush would drown in a lake in Alabama, and a former Marine with air-sea search and rescue training would be there to fish him out and perform CPR? Astronomical. As Roush later put it: "I liken the fact that I crashed into water rather than on land, that he was there and the boat was there, to winning one of these big state lotteries on three consecutive days with three separate tickets."

Once Hicks started to get to know Roush, he was amazed at the man's kindness. Sure, Jack was famous for his hard-nosed business dealings, but Roush has been kind to Larry and Donna, and the world has celebrated Roush's improving health.

"I've been impressed with how many people thought the world of Jack," Hicks says. "At Dover, people were yelling, 'Welcome back, God bless you!'"

Roush actually apologized to Hicks for the chaotic times after the rescue. Hicks laughed at the thought. Sure, he received plenty of live and phone interview requests from media members—including a writer named Tom Gillispie—and he's even called people back at his own expense.

But Hicks, who worked in public affairs before he retired in 1990, is a talker. He told his story again and again.

"It's hard to explain...Jack says he and I are tied together the rest of our lives because of the situation, and I'm inclined to agree," Hicks said. "You don't do something like this and not have it affect you. I look at him, and I look in a mirror. He should be dead. He had a one-in-20 chance of coming out alive, and he's had a remarkable recovery. It's amazing."

"I'm not a hero," he has said. "I was just in a position to help a guy out. I don't care about publicity. All I want is to know that he is going to be all right. I'm not a hero. I don't even think in those terms. I'm a husband, a father, and a grandfather. That's all."

Still, he had Roush's undying gratitude. Before Roush met Hicks, he was asked what he would do for the former Marine.

"I don't know what I'll do for Larry Hicks," Roush said, "but we've certainly got to think about him in our prayers." —T.G.

Bird Brain

A month or so before his death in 1993, Davey Allison said he saw a Dale Earnhardt fan up on the backstretch fence at Charlotte Motor Speedway. He was talking to crew chief Larry McReynolds on the radio at the time, and he was getting sick of the guy on the fence.

"You're going 200 miles an hour down the backstretch and you could tell he was an Earnhardt fan?" Allison was asked.

"Sure," he replied. "How could you tell?" "He was wearing an Earnhardt T-shirt and cap."

Allison paused a beat, then added: "You don't wait until you get there, because it would be a blur. You look ahead.

"Anyway, every time I'd come around the track, he'd throw me the bird, you know, the finger. It must have been about 20 laps, and I was getting tired of it. After a while, I got mad and threw him the bird back. He was so shocked, he fell off the fence." —T.G.

On the Spot

Cup driver Ken Schrader has a dry sense of humor.

Years ago, Keith Barnwell was spotting for Schrader on the Sonoma road course, now called Infineon Raceway, when he noticed that Schrader had gone into the dirt and a plume of dust had risen up. Then he realized that Schrader was coming up the hill end over end; eventually the car landed on its roof.

Barnwell asked Schrader how he was over the radio, and he reminded him not to unbuckle his belt before he got help lest he land on his head. Later, he found Ken in the care center. Again, he asked Schrader if he was okay. While the driver was dressing, he looked at Barnwell and solemnly said, "As the spotter, you've got to tell me when stuff like that is about to happen."

Right…like he could see the crash coming. —T.G.

Not Yet a Rookie

We were at Charlotte Motor Speedway in 2001, and Ryan Newman had just won the pole. The problem was what to *call* Newman. Newman was in his pre-rookie season; he would run seven races in 2001 so he could compete for rookie of the year in '02.

So was Newman a rookie or something else? Jerry Gappens, then the publicist at LMS (and now the boss of New Hampshire Motor Speedway), was smiling and asking.

I suggested proto-rookie or pre-rookie. Or premature rookie. We weren't sure.

As it turned out, Newman finished 43rd, last, in the Coca-Cola 600 that Sunday. That fall, he'd start fourth and finish 19th.

Going into the 2012 season, Newman had 15 Cup victories and a whopping 49 poles. So that "premature" pole in '01 was no fluke. —T.G.

chapter 13

Wonderboy

Jeff Gordon celebrates after winning Daytona 500, 2-20-05

Rick Hendrick was walking toward the suites
on the old frontstretch at Atlanta Motor Speedway—
it's the backstretch now—early in the 1992 season.
He noticed a car going through the turns smoking
its tires because the driver was pushing it so hard.

"Watch that car right there," Hendrick said
when he got to where he was going.
"He's getting ready to bust his tail."

But the car didn't wreck. It went to victory lane,
with Jeff Gordon driving it.

The following Monday, Hendrick was talking
about that driver at his team's shop in Charlotte.
It just so happened that one of
the guys working at the shop was sharing
an apartment with Gordon.

By the end of that year, Gordon was driving
a Winston Cup car for Hendrick Motorsports.
And one of the sport's greatest
careers was off and running.

Gordon Goes to School

Jeff Gordon might have been destined to be a stock car racing star all along, but the path he wound up taking went from California to Indiana to a venerable race track in the sandhills of North Carolina.

The outline of Gordon's pre-NASCAR story is widely known.

At age four, he lived in Vallejo, California, and wanted to race BMX bicycles. His mother, Carol, believed that was too dangerous, but somehow Jeff and his stepfather, John Bickford, convinced his mom that racing a quarter-midget race car would be safer.

By age eight, Gordon had won the national quarter-midget championship. He won it again at age 10 and established himself as a prodigy. In California, though, he couldn't race full-sized sprint cars until he was 18. In Indiana, though, he could move up at age 14.

So Bickford moved his family to Pittsboro, Indiana, and Jeff began racing in the United States Auto Club's (USAC's) national series at all of the tracks in and around Indiana where that kind of racing is done six or seven nights a week in the summer months.

Gordon remembers sitting in class during high school with the guy sitting beside him wearing a Jeff Gordon T-shirt he'd bought at one of those tracks. By 19, Gordon was the USAC national midget series champion. He was also one of the most talked-about young racers in America, thanks to a television show on ESPN called *Thursday Night Thunder*, which carried USAC races to a national cable television audience.

Bickford believed that television could help make his stepson a hot commodity, and he turned out to be exactly right. The Indianapolis-based production company behind *Thursday Night Thunder* came up with the idea to send Gordon to North Carolina Speedway in Rockingham, North Carolina. Buck Baker, the NASCAR legend, had a high-performance driving school that used the track for its classes, and the idea was to turn Jeff Gordon's first trip around a race track in a full-bodied stock car into a feature to air on the *Thursday Night Thunder* show.

What it did, however, was launch a career.

Gordon didn't know what all had been set up for him at Rockingham. Carol had to come with him because Gordon wasn't yet 21 and therefore couldn't rent a car to drive from the airport to the track. "Back in those days, they only told me what I needed to know," Gordon said.

He first went on the track in the school's regular cars. It was set up so the racers in training wouldn't be as likely to spin them around. But it was immediately clear that Gordon was too good for that.

"Buck came over to me after watching me a little bit and said, 'Would you like to get in that Busch car over there?'" Gordon recalled.

The Busch car belonged to Hugh Connerty, who'd been to Baker's school several times. Leo Jackson, who owned Harry Gant's Winston Cup team, was Connerty's father-in-law, and although Connerty was already 41, he still wanted to be a race car driver, too.

Connerty had bought a car Phil Barkdoll had used in Busch Series races. He kept it at Baker's school so that he could come up from his residence in Atlanta and keep trying to improve.

"Buck had called me up and asked me if I'd ever heard of Jeff Gordon," Connerty said. "I said, 'Sure, I've seen him on ESPN.' Buck wanted to know if I would come up and let Jeff drive my car."

So Connerty was there that day to see Gordon's first laps.

"I got in the car and I went pretty good," Gordon said. "We didn't have new tires on it, but I was a lot faster than Hugh was. He came up and said, 'Well, I've learned a lesson today. It's pretty obvious I shouldn't be driving that car.'"

Part of the legend of that day is that Gordon called home to Indiana and told Bickford to sell the sprint cars because he'd found his calling in stock cars.

At the very least, Connerty remembers Gordon's excitement.

"He flew out of the car like he'd won his first race," Connerty said.

Instead of driving the car himself in a few Busch races late in the 1990 season, Connerty put Gordon in the car. Gordon wanted to know who would be working on the car, and Connerty said that Andy Petree, who was Gant's crew chief on the team Connerty's father-in-law owned, had told him about a guy named Ray Evernham

Connerty called Evernham.

"I asked him, 'Have you ever heard of Jeff Gordon?'" Connerty said. "He said, 'Heck, yeah.'"

Connerty arranged for Evernham to come to Lowe's Motor Speedway near Charlotte for a test session. He also had to get Gordon signed, so Jackson gave Connerty a copy of

Gant's contract, minus the financial details, as a starting point. So, through Connerty, it was at a test in a Busch car that Evernham and Gordon—the team that would eventually win three Cup championships at Hendrick Motorsports—first met.

Evernham had Chuck Bown shake down the car at the test at Charlotte.

"When Jeff got in it, he took off," Evernham said. "He was flying. He came off one of the bumps in Turn 4 and got real loose in the car. I got on the radio and told him to bring it in. I said, 'Are you all right?' He didn't even know what I was asking him about."

Gordon entered the Charlotte Busch race in a No. 67 Pontiac sponsored by Outback Steakhouse (Connerty ran some restaurants in that franchise). But he wrecked in a qualifying race and didn't make the race.

The next race was at Rockingham. On October 18, 1990, Gordon ran 143.655 mph and qualified on the outside of Row 1 for the ACDelco 200 to be held the next day. He started in front of Dale Earnhardt, Darrell Waltrip, Mark Martin, and Davey Allison. Only Dave Mader, who won the pole at 143.915 mph, went faster.

"We were tight, tight, tight in practice," Evernham said. "We kept saying we needed to loosen the car up. Leo said he didn't think that was a good idea, but we did it anyway."

About 10 laps into the race, Gordon and Evernham understood what Jackson had been saying.

The car was so loose Gordon could barely get it around the track. He was holding on in the top 10, but on lap 34 he crashed on the backstretch. Gordon finished 39th. Steve Grissom won the race, with Earnhardt finishing second.

"After we wrecked," Evernham said, "Leo came up and said, 'The next time you won't worry about being tight, you'll worry about being tight enough.'" —D.P.

Gordon Pulling an Earnhardt

This was back before Darlington Raceway was flipped, and the press box was still in Turn 1. As always, I was sitting there beside *Winston Cup Scene* editor Deb Williams.

I noticed Dale Earnhardt do something interesting, and I had to tell someone.

Earnhardt, leading the race, came upon two lapped cars in Turn 1, and I figured he'd pass them on the backstretch. He didn't wait. He dove between the two cars in between Turns 1 and 2, a narrow stretch of road, and passed them in Turn 2. He was pulling away in the backstretch.

When she heard the story, Deb said, "That was Earnhardt being Earnhardt."

But that's not the end of the story. A few years later, Jeff Gordon was leading at Darlington and catching two lapped cars in the same turns, although they were probably then Turns 3 and 4. He dove between them and was soon pulling away.

I didn't tell Deb, but I guess that was Gordon being Earnhardt. —T.G.

A Car Is Declared Extinct

Over the course of NASCAR history, several cars have become infamous for the way they were built to test the edges of the rulebook.

Junior Johnson once built a Ford Galaxy with a chopped off roof and all kinds of twists and turns to its body so that it was nicknamed the "Yellow Banana." NASCAR allowed him to run it because Ford had been out of the sport for a while and the sanctioning body wanted it back in.

In 1987 Bill Elliott won just about every significant race held on the sport's bigger tracks. His No. 9 Ford was widely regarded to be a nearly perfectly "shrunk" version of the rest of the cars on the track—slightly smaller in almost every regard but not too small to fail NASCAR inspection.

One of the most famous cars in the sport's history ran in, and won, The Winston all-star race in 1997. Immediately afterward, NASCAR rewrote several rules to outlaw many of the things that made that car special.

Work on the car began shortly after car owner Rick Hendrick hired engineer Rex Stump in January 1996 and put him in charge of a research and development program for the team.

"It was kind of like our own 'Area 51,'" said Ray Evernham, who was Gordon's crew chief.

About a year later, Stump went to all of the various departments at the Hendrick shop and asked them to try to rethink the whole process of building race cars.

"We said 'If you had a blank sheet of paper, what would you do different in building a race car?'" Stump said. "It was something like 60 different people's ideas on how to make a better car."

Stump had studied what the NASCAR rulebook said—and what it didn't say, too—and figured that there was some wiggle room.

"It seemed we had a little more latitude as to what we could do," Stump said. "So we took it. Any place where there wasn't a rule, we took what we could."

The first time Hendrick saw what his R&D gang was up to, he looked underneath and around the car and said, "There's no way you're going to get to run this car." Hendrick made Stump and his group check in with NASCAR regularly during the car's construction to make sure he was wrong about that.

Generally speaking, the car had bigger frame rails that made the chassis "stiffer" and therefore more resistant to twisting forces as it went around the track. By moving elements in the suspension system as far "outboard" as possible, the car's geometry was also markedly different from existing Cup cars of the day. Every part's weight was carefully considered, as was how that weight was distributed.

As the car's on-track debut approached, it also picked up a nickname. The movie *The Lost World: Jurassic Park*, a sequel to the 1993 hit movie *Jurassic Park*, was about to come out, and the team made a deal to promote it with a special paint scheme. The car got a large dinosaur painted on its hood—a tyrannosaurus rex. Add that to Rex Stump's role in building it, and the car came to be called "T-Rex."

"The valence was pretty high up off the ground," Stump said, speaking of the things trained NASCAR eyes began to notice as soon as the car rolled out at Charlotte Motor Speedway to prepare for The Winston. "You'd walk down and see all the [other cars'] valences 3½ or 4 inches off the ground and this one was 5½ or 6 inches."

While the car sat higher off the ground, the opposite happened when it was going through the turns.

"It was built to 'land' in the middle of the corner to get all of the possible aero benefits, getting it as far down in front as possible and keeping the rear end up," Stump said.

That was a key to what made T-Rex special, Evernham said. "Everything was raised so that when you dropped the nose, it created negative pressure under the car," he said. It was a form of ground effects.

Gordon started 19th after messing up on his pit stop that was part of the qualifying format for the all-star event. But Gordon sliced through the field in the 30-lap first segment of The Winston before settling into third place. Dale Jarrett passed Dale Earnhardt on Lap 25 and won the segment.

Gordon lined up 16th when the field was inverted for the start of segment two. He was fourth, behind Bobby Labonte, Terry Labonte, and Ricky Craven, after those 30 laps, waiting for the right time to show all of his cards.

"I just remember that car being stuck to the track in a way that I had never felt a car be stuck before," he said. "It just gave me confidence, and it was fast—it was awesome."

It took him less than a lap and a half of the final 10-lap segment to take charge. He passed his teammate, Terry Labonte, for the lead and took off.

"When I got by Terry, I said, 'If this thing feels this good for the remainder of this thing, there's no way they can touch me.' We killed them. It was ridiculous."

Gordon had been, perhaps, too strong. His victory, combined with all of the attention the car had been getting before the race from competitors, assured the post-race inspection that night would be vigorous.

"When the race was over, I kind of knew there would be some moaning going on," Hendrick said.

It was more like howling.

"The other car owners looked at it and they all whined and flipped out and said, 'We'll have to build all new cars!'" Evernham said. "Everybody panicked. It's easier to kill Frankenstein than it is to figure out how to get along with him."

Gary Nelson, the man in charge of NASCAR's inspection process at the time, inspected the car before and after the race and said it was legal.

"Every detail of that car had been optimized," Nelson said. "None of it was outside the rules. We looked at the rulebook and there was nothing there that we could use to keep the car from racing. So we said, 'Let's let them race it and get to work on our rulebook.'"

After the race that night, NASCAR officials told Hendrick and Evernham that they should not plan on bringing the car back to race again.

"They said, 'Don't bring it back,'" Hendrick said. "I said, 'Hold on a minute. You can't tell me one week that it's okay and then the next week tell me not to bring it back!'"

Evernham also was aghast.

"I said, 'What? Why? It's legal,'" he said. "But they [NASCAR officials] kind of led me to believe that if I did bring it back it wasn't going to get through inspection, and we'd get every kind of pit-road penalty you could possibly have."

Hendrick asked NASCAR officials to come to the shop and take a closer look at the car to detail what they didn't like about it. "Maybe that was a mistake, because they spent a good bit of time really looking at the car," Stump said. "Then they went back and wrote a whole bunch of new rules that basically outlawed it."

Stump said at least a half-dozen specific rules were added to NASCAR's rulebook specifically to address issues raised by T-Rex. Nelson won't argue with that estimate.

Ultimately, the Hendrick team realized that if NASCAR wrote rules specific to what it could find in T-Rex, the team might still be able to use the things it hadn't found in its other cars. The team did race T-Rex again—in a state altered to appease NASCAR inspectors—later that year at Indianapolis. The changes hurt the car's performance, and Gordon finished only fourth, but Evernham said the process of building the car that won only once was still worthwhile.

"We learned stuff off of that car that we wound up using inside the new rules they wrote that have helped us on and on and on," Hendrick said. "That car paid big dividends." —D.P.

Getting Gordon's Goat

Jeff Gordon's first career Cup Series start came in the final race of the 1992 season at Atlanta Motor Speedway. Looking back now, it's noteworthy that Gordon's first start came in Richard Petty's last race.

At the drivers' meeting before that race, the Hooters 500, Petty gave each of the drivers who'd qualified for the race a commemorative money clip engraved with the name and date of the race along with the driver's name and his starting position. It also had the words, "Thanks for the Memories, Richard Petty," engraved on it.

Ty Norris, who later went on to work for Earnhardt at Dale Earnhardt Inc., was working for R.J. Reynolds at the time. He was at the drivers' meeting and saw his future boss get into a little mischief.

Gordon, Norris said, was paying rapt attention to the drivers' meeting. Now, the typical drivers' meeting is very much like the safety lecture at the start of an airplane flight. After a while, the passengers could recite it. But this was Gordon's Cup debut, and he didn't want to miss anything.

"He was sitting next to Dale," Norris said. "They're going through all the procedures, and Gordon's just focused in on whoever was talking. He was just staring at them, not like a lot of the drivers who are looking around or staring at their watches."

Earnhardt, seeing Gordon so into what was being said at the front of the room, reached off and slipped Gordon's money clip away. Gordon never saw a thing.

"Everybody was finished, and they were walking up to Richard shaking his hand and thanking him," Norris said. "Jeff walked out of the meeting and suddenly remembered he'd forgotten something. He went back to his seat to look for it, but it wasn't there. He was running around looking for it.

"Dale was about to fall on the floor laughing. Finally, he walked over to Gordon and said, 'You need to pay attention, kid, this is a pretty big deal.'" —D.P.

Report to Your Car

We were in the Benny Kahn infield press room at Daytona, with a very young Jeff Gordon sitting in a chair on the dais. He was sitting with his legs straight out and looked maybe 12 or 13 years old.

Suddenly, a stout voice came over the loud speaker: "Jeff Gordon, report to your car. Jeff Gordon, report to your car."

Gordon sat up and said something like, "I'm sorry, guys. I gotta go. They're calling for me."

As Gordon walked between the tables of reporters toward the door, Darrell Waltrip strode in. DW, the next man on the program, had a broad grin, and it was obvious that he was the one who had called for Jeff to leave.

I always wondered if Jeff realized what Waltrip had pulled on him. —T.G.

A Little Help, Jeff

In 2004, the *Charlotte Observer* allowed me to spend most of the month of June covering different styles of racing off the NASCAR beat. One of the races I attended was the U.S. Grand Prix, a Formula One race at Indianapolis Motor Speedway.

During the week of that race, I was invited to a dinner with some officials of the Toyota F1 team. At this dinner, the conversation inevitably turned to the argument of whether having a competitive American driver in the world's most significant racing series would make F1 more popular in this country, where it has only a loyal but smaller niche following.

As the evening ended, an official with Toyota handed me his business card. "If you come across a good, young American driver who you think could make it in Formula One, you give him this card and have him call me," he said.

I kept the card until I went back onto the NASCAR beat for the July 4 weekend race at Daytona International Speedway.

On the first day of practice, I asked Jon Edwards, Gordon's outstanding public relations man, to get me five minutes with Gordon. And I told Jon he needed to be there, too.

After a practice session, I walked up into the back of the No. 24 team's hauler with Gordon and Edwards. Both are big F1 fans, so it wasn't any problem getting that topic brought up.

I told Gordon about the dinner with the Toyota folks. I told him about the business card and I pulled it out my pocket.

You have to realize that about twice each year since Gordon has been a NASCAR star, somebody has started a rumor saying that he might leave stock car racing to go drive an F1 car. He actually tested one at Indy, in a PR stunt for the track in which he and Juan Pablo Montoya "switched" cars for a few laps.

"Jeff," I said, "this gentleman told me to get this card to an outstanding young American driver who might have a future in F1."

Gordon smiled.

And then, I got my punch line out.

"Could you please give this card to Jimmie Johnson for me?" I asked.

Edwards nearly fell in the floor laughing. —D.P.

chapter 14
Young Guns

Carl Edwards does backflip after winning the NASCAR Busch Aaron's 312, 3-19-05

Jeff Gordon's success in NASCAR convinced a lot of people that young drivers could get the job done, and get it done well. Gordon won 55 races before his 30th birthday. Only Richard Petty, with 60, won more before turning 30.

In the years since Gordon's arrival, these young drivers have begun to make their own mark on the sport. None of them has quite matched Gordon's early career pace, but they've done all right for themselves.

That Carl Edwards—He's a Card

It's not exactly "Will Work for Food," but it's close.

Carl Edwards exploded onto the Cup racing scene in 2005, earning his first victory in NASCAR's top series at Atlanta Motor Speedway in just the fourth race of his first full season as driver for car owner Jack Roush.

He passed Jimmie Johnson off the final turn on the final lap to get that victory, just one day after he'd earned his first career victory in the Busch Nationwide Series at the same track.

After both wins, Edwards did back flips off the window sill of his race car. The celebration was something he saw an open-wheel driver do once, and Edwards thought it was cool. So he copied the move when he started winning races in NASCAR's Truck Series. Now, it has become his trademark.

Edwards is unique, there's no question about that. He came into stock car racing's top series with a wide-eyed exuberance that quickly endeared him to NASCAR fans.

The story of how Edwards got to The Cup Series is unique, too.

His father, Carl "Mike" Edwards, owned a Volkswagen repair shop and won more than 200 features in various forms of racing around the Midwest. Carl Jr. followed in those footsteps, beginning his career in four-cylinder VWs at the age of 14.

Edwards' father is a cousin of NASCAR driver Ken Schrader, and when Carl Jr. was 17, he went to work in Schrader's shop.

"That kind of turned racing into a reality for me," Edwards says. "I was mowing the grass at the shop and going to the races and helping out, and I realized these guys were all just guys who go racing at home every week, just at a different level. I went home and decided it was time to get going, to learn how to race."

He drove dirt-track modifieds and won track championships at Capital Speedway in Holt Summit, Missouri, in 1999 and 2000, then moved on to the U.S. Auto Club's Silver Crown Series.

All the while, Edwards was looking for a way to get his foot into the door in NASCAR. He had a friend who was an aspiring actor, and that friend had a card with his photograph and biographical information on it that he could hand out at auditions.

"So I thought, 'Man, I need to get a card or some sort of piece of information that I can give to people,'" Edwards said. "I sat down and talked to my mom [Nancy Sterling] about it, and she said, 'You need a business card. You need a business card that says you want to drive race cars.' And I thought, 'Man, that's great!'"

Edwards went to a print shop in his hometown of Columbia, Missouri.

"They gave me a great deal," he said. "It was like $100 for 2,000 business cards with my picture on them and everything on it. My whole resume was on the back—not in very small print either—but I had a resume and I just started handing them out to everyone. I think I passed out 2,500 of them.

"Everywhere I went I always had business cards. I figured eventually the whole world would know that I wanted to drive race cars and there would be some owner that would need a driver and somebody would say, 'Man, you ought to hire him!'"

After Edwards arrived on the Cup scene, fellow driver Tony Stewart talked about seeing the card that Edwards had printed in the classified ads section of *National Speed Sport News*, laughing at the idea that anybody thought that might work.

But in 2002, Edwards got his shot. He made seven starts for a Truck Series team owned by Mike Mittler, getting only one top-10 finish.

But he did well enough with a team that was fighting uphill financially to get noticed by some of the folks at Roush Racing, who were about to unexpectedly need a Truck Series driver for the 2003 season.

Roush planned to put Kyle Busch in a truck that season once Busch reached his 18th birthday in May. But before the season started, Busch signed to drive at Hendrick Motorsports, leaving Roush with a team but no driver.

So a door opened for Edwards, and he walked through it. Edwards won three races and took rookie of the year honors. He won three more Truck races in 2004, and when Jeff Burton left the No. 99 team to jump to Richard Childress Racing, Roush put Edwards into that car.

"Everything just worked out perfectly," Edwards said. "I had a lot of really good people. My mom and her husband, Jim Sterling, are unbelievable. They've helped me so much. My mom has always been my backbone and supported me so much. My dad is the smartest racer in the world, and I feel like the things I do on the race track and the way that I approach racing is because of my father."

After the victory at Atlanta, Edwards surprised his mother by buying her a new car.

Life, in other words, is good.

"Just look at what we're doing," Edwards said. "It's the neatest thing in the world....We get to go out there and drive as hard as we can and think as hard as we can about how to make the cars faster. You're competing against other human beings, which is the neatest thing in the world. We get to go out there and risk it all and race for glory and all that. It's the most fun thing in the world. It's just awesome. I mean, this is as good as it gets. It's unbelievable, and I'm enjoying every minute of it." —D.P.

Working for a Living

Sometimes, people actually do have a "Eureka!" moment.

It's an instant when the picture becomes clear and they understand where they want to go with their lives. It happened, for instance, to Sprint Cup championship-winning driver Tony Stewart.

"I was working at a machine shop for $5 an hour in the middle of the country in Rush County, Indiana," Stewart said. "I sat in a big barn on a metal stool on a concrete floor at a drill press and was picking up parts out of a 5-gallon bucket full of solvent.

"It was a good thing I actually started the job before winter came because I knew the roads good enough. You had to blow through the snow drifts just to get to and from work."

Stewart also had been driving race cars ever since he was a boy growing up in Columbus, Indiana, where he'd convinced the owner of the local Dairy Queen to sponsor his go-karts by letting him have free chocolate milk shakes. Stewart was racing midgets and sprint cars by the time he had the job in the machine shop, and he was good, too.

That winter, he took a USAC Silver Crown division car to the Copper World Classic in Phoenix and finished second to Mike Bliss.

"My portion of the prize money was, like, $3,500," Stewart said. "When I came back to work on Monday, I was sitting at that drill press and started trying to figure out how many $5 hours I had to work to make $3,500.

"I thought, 'When I drive race cars I can get up at noon. I'm at the pit gate by 4:00. I'm done at midnight, and I'm still wide awake. If I can do that three nights a week and pay my bills I don't have to get up at 7:30 and drive to work and work five days a week."

Eureka! —D.P.

Gone, but Not Forgotten

About six weeks before the 2001 NASCAR season began, Dale Earnhardt Jr. sat in front of the media and talked about a dream he'd had.

He dreamed about the 2001 Daytona 500—and about winning it. "I was out front all day," he said of the dream. "I kept telling myself I won it in my second time in the race."

His father had won the 500 in 1998 and was the acclaimed master of racing on NASCAR's restrictor-plate tracks.

Somebody asked Earnhardt Jr. where Dale Earnhardt's black No. 3 Chevrolet was in the dream.

"Dad," Earnhardt Jr. said, "wasn't there."

Those words took on an eerie feel on February 19.

On the final lap of the Daytona 500, Earnhardt Jr. wasn't exactly out front. He was second, running behind new teammate Michael Waltrip.

Earnhardt was there, running third right behind the two cars his Dale Earnhardt Inc. team owned.

But then, he was gone.

The images flash in the memories of race fans everywhere.

A crash in Turn 4. Earnhardt's car snapping up the track and running into the outside wall with frightening force. Ken Schrader jumping out of his car, which had rammed into the side of the black No. 3 an instant before it nosed into the wall, and running to check on his friend and rival. An ambulance carrying Earnhardt leaving the track slowly, much too slowly.

And then, the awful news.

Dale Earnhardt, who had for so long seemed so indestructible, had been killed.

It didn't seem possible. As difficult as it was for the fans to believe, imagine how hard his father's death was for Earnhardt Jr. to understand. Of all the things Earnhardt Jr. ever wanted to achieve in a race car, earning his father's respect was right at the top of that list.

"It's like a never-ending process," Earnhardt Jr. said of his efforts to do that. "It's bottomless. I get worn out by it at times. But it's something you always want. Sometimes it becomes more important than the job at hand. What other reason do you race for? You race for thousands of dollars. That's good. You race to win. That's good. Those are good reasons. But there's nothing wrong with wanting to make my dad happy."

And then, he was gone.

"I thought he was Superman," Earnhardt Jr. said.

Five months later, Earnhardt Jr. had to come back to Daytona to race again. The Pepsi 400 in July would be one of the most emotional races of his young life, no matter how well he ran. And when Earnhardt Jr. won the race, it was one of the most emotional moments the sport has ever known.

Earnhardt Jr. had come to Daytona a couple of days early that summer. He went down in Turn 4, near the spot where his father had crashed. He sat there, thinking about all he'd seen his father do and all he'd learned from watching it. And he made a kind of peace with Daytona. His dad had loved racing there. Earnhardt had cherished all of his many successes at Daytona, and he absolutely reveled in his victory in the Daytona 500 in 1998 that had ended a career filled with frustration.

"In a way, it feels like I'm closer to Dad when [I'm] here," Earnhardt Jr. said of Daytona. "But at the same time, you get reminded of losing him all over again."

Earnhardt Jr. had begun to show prowess on restrictor-place tracks that reminded everyone of his father, but, like his dad, he'd missed out on a couple of potential opportunities to win the Daytona 500.

"There are days when I feel like I am as good as he was," Earnhardt Jr. said. "But then you're reminded by something that reminds you of what he did that you'll never be able to do. There are times on the track where I get real confident and fee like I couldn't have done it any better than that right there. Bu it's not long before I figure out I'm wrong.

"He was pretty tough. You have to watch some old t to see things he did on the track to remind you how sli was and how determined he was. He always figured it out, you know?"

But in February 2004, Earnhardt Jr. got a victory in NASCAR's biggest race. It was a memorable day, beginning with President George W. Bush flying in on Air Force One before the race to participate in the ceremonies before the start of another season. The president actually called the start of the race in the Motor Racing Network's radio booth, with long-time play-by-play announcer Barney Hall giving an assist.

After the race, as he stood in the press box doing his post-race interviews, someone handed Earnhardt Jr. a cell phone. The president, who'd left during the race, was calling to say congratulations.

It had taken his father 20 tries to win the Daytona 500. Earnhardt Jr. did it in his fifth.

"He was over in the passenger seat riding with me," Earnhardt Jr. said of his late father. "I'm sure he was having a blast."

That wasn't the last time Earnhardt Jr. felt his father's presence around him in a race car. In July 2004, during a weekend off on the Nextel Cup schedule, Earnhardt Jr. went to Infineon Raceway road course to compete in an American ᵔs Series race with a factory-backed Chevrolet team. In ᵔ session on the morning of the race, Earnhardt Jr. ᵔ the car erupted in flames.

ᵔarnhardt Jr. managed to unbuckle himself and ᵔe suffered burns that forced him to get ᵔbsequent Cup races, but he survived. ᵔpital on that day, Earnhardt Jr. ᵔl Steve Crisp, who'd gone with him to

California for that race, and told Crisp that he had to find "the guy who pulled me out of the car."

Crisp told Earnhardt Jr. that nobody had pulled him out.

At first, Earnhardt Jr. didn't say much about what had happened—and about what he thought had happened. But several months later, he recalled what he felt while he was in that fire.

"I reached up into the roll bar to pull myself out, somebody grabbed me underneath the arms, I thought, and pulled me out of the car," Earnhardt Jr. said. "It was as real as [it could be]. It was no dream or whatever. Call me crazy; I don't care. That was an experience that only I know and only I can tell it.

"I swear somebody had me underneath my arms and was carrying me out of the car," Earnhardt Jr. said. "I mean, I swear to God."

Earnhardt Jr. told that story for the first time in an interview on *60 Minutes* with famed journalist Mike Wallace.

"And that was your dad?" Wallace asked.

"I don't know," Earnhardt Jr. said. "You tell me. It freaks me just talking about it. It just gives me chills." —D.P.

sources

Chapin, Kim. *Fast as White Lightning.* New York: Dial Press, 1981.

Cutter, Robert and Fendell, Bob. *Encyclopedia of Auto Racing Greats.* Englewood Cliffs, NJ: Prentice-Hall, 1973.

Engel, Lyle Kenyon. *Stock Car Racing USA.* New York: Dodd, Mead and Co., 1973.

Fielden, Greg. *High Speed at Low Tide.* Surfside Beach, SC: Galfied Press, 1993.

Fielden, Greg. *Forty Years of Stock Car Racing: Vol. I, The Beginning 1949–1958.* Pinehurst, NC: Garfield Press, 1988.

Fielden, Greg. *Forty Years of Stock Car Racing: Vol. II, The Speedway Boom, 1959–1964.* Pinehurst, NC: Garfield Press, 1988.

Fielden, Greg. *Forty Years of Stock Car Racing: Vol. III, Big Bucks and Boycotts, 1965–1971.* Pinehurst, NC: Garfield Press, 1988.

Fielden, Greg. *Forty Years of Stock Car Racing: Vol. IV, The Modern Era, 1972–1989.* Pinehurst, NC: Garfield Press, 1988.

Fielden, Greg. *Rumblin' Ragtops: The History of NASCAR's Fabulous Convertible Division.* Pinehurst, NC: Garfield Press, 1990.

Golenbock, Peter. *American Zoom: Stock Car Racing–From the Dirt Tracks to Daytona.* New York: McMillan Publishing Co., 1993.

Higgins, Tom. *That's Racin'.com, Tom Higgins' Scuffs.* Knight Ridder Digital, Sept. 15, 2005.

Higgins, Tom and Waid, Steve. *Junior Johnson, Brave in Life.* Phoenix, AZ: David Bull Publishing, 1999.

⌐r, Jim. *Darlington Raceway 50ᵗʰ Anniversary.* Charlotte, NC: UMI ¹ications, 1999.

ᵀᵐ. *NASCAR's Most Wanted: The Top 10 Book of ⌐s Drivers, Wild Wrecks, and Other Oddities.* Washington, ᵥ's, 2001.

⌐d Neely, William. *Cale: The Hazardous Life and ⌐′s Greatest Stock Car Driver.* New York: Times

⌐ᵢ Sons-a-Bitches, Let's Have a Race! ⌐ Press, 2001.